1st ed 1935   £2-00
Ex Jacobs
£5

THE WORKING CLASS AGAINST FASCISM

GEORGI DIMITROV

G. Dimitrov

THE WORKING CLASS AGAINST FASCISM

London

MARTIN LAWRENCE

FIRST PUBLISHED NOVEMBER 1935

The present work comprises the official text of the Report and the two speeches delivered by G. DIMITROV, *General Secretary of the Communist International, at that body's Seventh World Congress, held in Moscow in August* 1935.

PRINTED AT THE FARLEIGH PRESS, E.C.I
AND PUBLISHED BY MARTIN LAWRENCE LTD.
33, GREAT JAMES STREET, LONDON, W.C.I

Contents

PAGE

THE REPORT 9

The Class Character of Fascism 10

What does Victorious Fascism Bring for the Masses? 14

Is the Victory of Fascism Inevitable? 17

Fascism—a Ferocious but Unstable Power ... 23

II. UNITED FRONT OF THE WORKING CLASS AGAINST FASCISM 28

Importance of the United Front 28

The Chief Arguments of the Opponents of the United Front... 29

Content and Forms of the United Front 32

The Anti-Fascist People's Front 35

Cardinal Questions of the United Front in Individual Countries 37

(a) The United States of America 37

(b) Great Britain 39

(c) France 40

The United Front and the Fascist Mass Organisations 43

The United Front in the Countries where the Social-Democrats are in Office 48

The Struggle for Trade Union Unity 53

The United Front and the Youth 58

Women and the United Front 60

The Anti-Imperialist United Front 61

The Government of the United Front 62

The Ideological Struggle Against Fascism ... 68

III. CONSOLIDATION OF THE COMMUNIST PARTIES AND STRUGGLE FOR THE POLITICAL UNITY OF THE PROLETARIAT 74

Consolidation of the Communist Parties 74

Political Unity of the Working Class 78

CONCLUSION 82

SPEECH IN REPLY TO DISCUSSION 85

    The Struggle Against Fascism Must be Made
       Concrete 87

    The United Proletarian Front and the Anti-Fascist
       People's Front 90

    The Role of Social-Democracy and its Attitude
       Towards the United Front of the Proletariat ... 93

    The United Front Government 96

    Attitude Towards Bourgeois Democracy 98

    A Correct Line Alone is Not Enough 100

    Cadres 104

SPEECH CONCLUDING THE CONGRESS 117

Dimitrov's Report

Comrades, as early as its Sixth Congress, the Communist International warned the world proletariat that a new fascist offensive was impending, and called for a struggle against it. The Congress pointed out that " in a more or less developed form, fascist tendencies and the germs of a fascist movement are to be found almost everywhere."

With the outbreak of the present most profound economic crisis, the sharp accentuation of the general crisis of capitalism and the revolutionisation of the toiling masses, fascism has embarked upon a wide offensive. The ruling bourgeoisie is more and more seeking salvation in fascism, with the object of instituting exceptionally predatory measures against the toilers, preparing for an imperialist war of plunder, attacking the Soviet Union, enslaving and partitioning China, and by all these means preventing revolution.

Imperialist circles are endeavouring to place the *whole* burden of the crisis on the backs of the toilers. *That is why they need fascism.*

They are trying to solve the problem of markets by enslaving the weak nations, by intensifying colonial oppression and repartitioning the world anew by means of war. *That is why they need fascism.*

They are striving to *forestall* the growth of the forces of revolution by smashing the revolutionary movement of the workers and peasants and by undertaking a military attack against the Soviet Union—the bulwark of the world proletariat. *That is why they need fascism.*

In a number of countries, Germany in particular, these imperialist circles have succeeded, *before* the masses have decisively turned towards revolution, in inflicting defeat on the proletariat and establishing a fascist dictatorship.

But what is characteristic of the victory of fascism is the fact that this victory, on the one hand, bears witness to the weakness of the proletariat, disorganised and paralysed by the disruptive Social-Democratic policy of class collaboration with the bourgeoisie, and, on the other, expresses the weakness of the bourgeoisie itself, afraid of

the realisation of a united struggle of the working class,
afraid of revolution, and no longer in a position to maintain its dictatorship over the masses by the old methods of
bourgeois democracy and parliamentarism.

The victory of fascism in Germany, Comrade Stalin said
at the Seventeenth Congress of the Communist Party of
the Soviet Union,

" must be regarded not only as a symptom of the weakness of the
working class and as a result of the betrayal of the working class
by Social-Democracy, which paved the way for fascism; it must
also be regarded as a symptom of the weakness of the bourgeoisie,
as a symptom of the fact that the bourgeoisie is already unable
to rule by the old methods of parliamentarism and bourgeois
democracy, and, as a consequence, is compelled in its home policy
to resort to terroristic methods of administration—it must be taken
as a symptom of the fact that it is no longer able to find a way
out of the present situation on the basis of a peaceful foreign
policy, as a consequence of which it is compelled to resort to a
policy of war."

The Class Character of Fascism.

Comrades, as was correctly stated by the Thirteenth
Plenum of the Executive Committee of the Communist
International, fascism in power is *the open terrorist dictatorship of the most reactionary, most chauvinistic and
most imperialist elements of finance capital.*

The most reactionary variety of fascism is *the German
type* of fascism. It has the effrontery to call itself National-
Socialism, though having nothing in common with
Socialism. Hitler fascism is not only bourgeois
nationalism, it is bestial chauvinism. It is a government
system of political banditry, a system of provocation and
torture practised upon the working class and the revolutionary elements of the peasantry, the petty bourgeoisie and
the intelligentsia. It is medieval barbarity and bestiality
in its own country, it is unbridled aggression in relation to
other nations and countries.

German fascism is acting as *the spearhead of international counter-revolution, as the chief incendiary of imperialist war,* as *the initiator of a crusade against the Soviet
Union, the great fatherland of the toilers of the whole world.*

Fascism is not a form of State power " standing above
both classes—the proletariat and the bourgeoisie," as Otto
Bauer, for instance, has asserted. It is not " the revolt
of the lower middle-class which has seized the machinery

of the State," as the British Socialist Brailsford declares. No, fascism is not super-class government, nor government of the petty bourgeoisie or the lumpenproletariat over finance capital. Fascism is the power of finance capital itself. It is the organisation of terrorist vengeance against the working class and the revolutionary section of the peasantry and intelligentsia. In foreign policy, fascism is chauvinism in its crudest form, fomenting bestial hatred of other nations.

This, the true character of fascism, must be particularly stressed; because in a number of countries fascism, under cover of social demagogy, has managed to gain the following of the petty-bourgeois masses who have been driven out of their course by the crisis, and even of certain sections of the most backward strata of the proletariat. These would never have supported fascism if they had understood its real class character and its true nature.

The development of fascism, and of the fascist dictatorship itself, assumes *different forms* in different countries, according to historical, social and economic conditions and to the national peculiarities and the international position of the given country. In certain countries, principally those in which fascism does not enjoy a broad mass basis and in which the struggle of the various groups within the camp of the fascist bourgeoisie itself is fairly acute, fascism does not immediately venture to abolish parliament, but allows the other bourgeois parties, as well as the Social-Democratic parties, to retain a certain degree of legality. In other countries, where the ruling bourgeoisie fears an *early* outbreak of revolution, fascism has established its unrestricted political monopoly, either immediately or by intensifying its reign of terror against and persecution of all competing parties and groups. This does not prevent fascism, when its position becomes *particularly* acute, from endeavouring to extend its basis and without altering its class nature, *combining* open terrorist dictatorship with a crude sham of parliamentarism.

The accession to power of fascism is not an *ordinary succession* of one bourgeois government by another, but a *substitution* for one State form of class domination of the bourgeoisie—bourgeois democracy—of another form—open terrorist dictatorship. It would be a serious mistake to ignore this distinction, a mistake which would prevent the of bourgeois reaction, *fascism adapts* its demagogy to the national *peculiarities* of each country, and even to the peculiarities of the various social strata in one and the same country. And the petty-bourgeois masses, even a section of the workers, reduced to despair by want, unemployment and the insecurity of their existence, fall victim to the social and chauvinist demagogy of fascism.

Fascism comes to power as a *party of attack* on the revolutionary movement of the proletariat, on the masses of the people who are in a state of unrest; yet it stages its accession to power as a " revolutionary " movement against the bourgeoisie on behalf of " the whole nation " and for " the salvation " of the nation. (Let us recall Mussolini's " march " on Rome, Pilsudski's " march " on Warsaw, Hitler's National-Socialist " revolution " in Germany, and so forth.)

But whatever the masks which fascism adopts, whatever the forms in which it presents itself, whatever the ways by which it comes to power—

fascism is a most ferocious attack by capital on the toiling masses;

fascism is unbridled chauvinism and annexationist war;

fascism is rabid reaction and counter-revolution;

fascism is the most vicious enemy of the working class and of all the toilers!

What Does Victorious Fascism Bring for the Masses?

Fascism promised the workers " a fair wage," but actually it has brought them to an even lower, a pauper standard of living. It promised work for the unemployed, but actually has brought them even more painful torments of starvation, and compulsory, servile labour. It actually converts the workers and unemployed into pariahs of capitalist society stripped of rights, destroys their trade unions; deprives them of the right to strike and to have their working class press, forces them into fascist organisations, plunders their social insurance funds and transforms the mills and factories into barracks where the unbridled arbitrary rule of the capitalists prevails.

Fascism promised the toiling *youth* a broad highway to a brilliant future. But actually it has brought with it wholesale dismissals of young workers, labour camps and continuous military drilling for a war of conquest.

Fascism promised the *non-manual workers, the petty officials and the intellectuals* to ensure them security of existence, to destroy the omnipotence of the trusts and wipe out profiteering by bank capital. But actually it has brought them an even greater degree of hopelessness and uncertainty as to the morrow; it is subjecting them to a new bureaucracy made up of the most compliant of its followers, it is setting up an intolerable dictatorship of the trusts, and fosters corruption and degeneration to an unprecedented extent.

Fascism promised the ruined and impoverished *peasants* to put an end to debt bondage, to abolish rent and even to alienate the landed estates without compensation, in the interests of the landless and impoverished peasants. But actually it is placing the toiling peasants in a state of unprecedented servitude to the trusts and the fascist state apparatus, and promotes the exploitation of the great mass of the peasantry by the big agrarians, the banks and the usurers to the very utmost limit.

" Germany will be a peasant country, or will not be at all," Hitler solemnly declared. And what did the peasants of Germany get under Hitler? A moratorium, which has already been cancelled? Or a law on the inheritance of peasant property, which is resulting in millions of sons and daughters of peasants being squeezed out of the villages and reduced to paupers? Farm labourers have been transformed into semi-serfs deprived even of the elementary right of free movement. Toiling peasants have been deprived of the opportunity of selling the produce of their farms in the market.

And in Poland?

" The Polish peasant," says the Polish newspaper *Czas,* " employs methods and means which were used perhaps only in the Middle Ages : he nurses the fire in his stove and lends it to his neighbour; he splits matches into several parts; he lends dirty soap-water to others; he boils herring barrels in order to obtain salt water. This is not a fable, but the actual state of affairs in the countryside, of the truth of which anybody may convince himself."

And it is not Communists who write this, comrades, but a Polish reactionary newspaper !

But this is by no means all.

Every day, in the concentration camps of fascist Germany, in the cellars of the Gestapo (German secret police), in the torture chambers of Poland, in the cells of the Bulgarian and Finnish secret police, in the " Glavnyacha " in Belgrade, in the Rumanian " Siguranza," and on the Italian islands, some of the best sons of the working class, revolutionary peasants, fighters for the splendid future of mankind, are being subjected to revolting tortures and indignities, in comparison with which the most abominable acts of the Tsarist secret police are relatively mild.   The villainous German fascists beat husbands to a bloody pulp in the presence of their wives, and send the ashes of murdered sons by parcel post to their mothers.   Sterilisation has been made a method of political warfare.   In the torture chambers, captured antifascists are given injections of poison, their arms are broken, their eyes gouged out; they are strung up and have water pumped into them ; the fascist swastika is carved in their living flesh.

I have before me a statistical summary drawn up by the International Red Aid—the international organisation for aid to revolutionary fighters—regarding the number of killed, wounded, arrested, maimed and tortured to death in Germany, Poland, Italy, Austria, Bulgaria, Yugoslavia.   In Germany alone, since the National-Socialists came to power, over 4,200 anti-fascist workers, peasants, employees, intellectuals—Communists, Social-Democrats and members of opposition Christian organisations—have been murdered, 317,800 arrested, 218,600 wounded and subjected to excruciating tortures.   In Austria, since the battles of February last year, the " Christian " fascist government has murdered 1,900 revolutionary workers, maimed and wounded 10,000, and arrested 40,000.   And this summary, comrades, is far from complete.

Words fail me in describing the indignation which seizes us at the thought of the torments which the toilers are now suffering in a number of fascist countries.   The facts and figures we quote *do not reflect one-hundredth part of the true picture* of the exploitation and the tortures inflicted by the White Terror which make up the daily life of the working class in many capitalist countries.   Volumes cannot give a just picture of the countless brutalities inflicted by fascism on the toilers.

With feelings of profound emotion and hatred for the fascist butchers, we lower the banners of the Communist International before the unforgettable memory of John Scheer, Fiete   Schulz   and   Lüttgens   in   Germany,   Koloman Wallisch   and   Münichreiter   in   Austria,   Sallai   and Fürst in Hungary, Kofardzhiev, Lutibrodsky and Voikov in Bulgaria—before the memory of thousands and thousands of Communists, Social-Democrats and non-party workers, peasants and representatives of the progressive intelligentsia who have laid down their lives in the struggle against fascism. From this platform we greet the leader of the German proletariat and the honorary chairman of our Congress—Comrade Thälmann. We greet Comrades Rakosi, Gramsci, Antikainen and J. Panov. We greet the leader of the Spanish Socialists, Caballero, imprisoned by the counter-revolutionaries; Tom Mooney, who has been languishing in prison for eighteen years, and the thousands of other prisoners of capitalism and fascism, and we say to them : " Brothers in the fight, brothers in arms, you are not forgotten. We are with you. We shall give every hour of our lives, every drop of our blood, for your liberation, and for the liberation of all toilers, from the shameful regime of fascism."

Comrades, it was Lenin who warned us that the bourgeoisie may succeed in overwhelming the toilers by savage terror, in checking the growing forces of revolution for brief periods of time, but that, nevertheless, this would not save it from its doom.

" Life," Lenin wrote, " will assert itself. Let the bourgeoisie rave, work itself into a frenzy, overdo things, commit stupidities, take vengeance in advance on the Bolsheviks and endeavour to kill off (in India, Hungary, Germany, etc.), extra hundreds, thousands, and hundreds of thousands of yesterday's or to-morrow's Bolsheviks. Acting thus, the bourgeoisie acts as all classes doomed to destruction by history have acted. Communists should know that at all events the future belongs to them ; and therefore we can, and must, combine the most intense passion in the great revolutionary struggle with the coolest and most sober estimation of the frenzied convulsions of the bourgeoisie."*

Aye, if we and the proletariat of the whole world firmly follow the path indicated by Lenin and Stalin, the bourgeoisie will perish in spite of everything.

Is the Victory of Fascism Inevitable?

Why was it that fascism could triumph, and how ?

Fascism is the most vicious enemy of the working class and the toilers. Fascism is the enemy of nine-tenths of the German people, nine-tenths of the Austrian people, nine-tenths of the other peoples in fascist countries. How, in what way, could this vicious enemy triumph ?

Fascism was able to come to power *primarily* because the working class, owing to the policy of class collaboration with

---

* Lenin, " *Left-Wing* " *Communism, an Infantile Disorder*, pp. 100-01.

the bourgeoisie pursued by Social-Democratic leaders, *proved to be split, politically and organisationally disarmed,* in face of the onslaught of the bourgeoisie. And the Communist Parties, on the other hand, were *not strong enough* to be able, apart from and in the teeth of the Social-Democrats, to rouse the masses and to lead them in a decisive struggle against fascism.

And, indeed, let the millions of Social-Democratic workers, who, together with their Communist brothers, are now experiencing the horrors of fascist barbarism, seriously reflect on this. If in 1918, when revolution broke out in Germany and Austria, the Austrian and German proletariat had not followed the Social-Democratic leadership of Otto Bauer, Friedrich Adler and Karl Renner in Austria, and Ebert and Schiedemann in Germany, but had followed the road of the Russian Bolsheviks, the road of Lenin and Stalin, there would now be no fascism in Austria or Germany, in Italy or Hungary, in Poland or in the Balkans. Not the bourgeoisie but the working class would long ago have been the master of the situation in Europe.

Take, for example, the *Austrian* Social-Democratic Party. The revolution of 1918 raised it to a tremendous height. It held power in its hands, it held strong positions in the army and in the State apparatus. Relying on these positions, it could have nipped fascism in the bud. But it surrendered one position of the working class after another without resistance. It permitted the bourgeoisie to strengthen its power, annul the constitution, purge the State apparatus, army and police force of Social-Democratic functionaries, and take the arsenals away from the workers. It allowed the fascist bandits to murder Social-Democratic workers with impunity and accepted the terms of the Hüttenberg pact, which gave the fascist elements entry to the factories. At the same time the Social-Democratic leaders fooled the workers with the Linz programme, in which the alternative was provided for the possibility of using armed force against the bourgeoisie and for the establishment of a proletarian dictatorship, assuring them that in the event of the ruling classes using force against the working class, the party would reply by a call for a general strike and for armed struggle. As though the whole policy of preparation for a fascist attack on the working class were not one chain of acts of violence against the working class masked by constitutional forms. Even on the eve and in the course of the February battles the Austrian Social Democratic leaders left the heroically fighting Schutzbund isolated from the broad masses and doomed the Austrian proletariat to defeat.

Was the victory of fascism inevitable in *Germany*?   No, the German working class could have prevented it.

But in order to do so, it should have compelled the establishment of a united anti-fascist proletarian front, forced the Social-Democratic leaders to put a stop to their campaign against the Communists and to accept the repeated proposals of the Communist Party for united action against fascism.

When fascism was on the offensive and the bourgeois-democratic liberties were being progressively abolished by the bourgeoisie, it should not have contented itself with the verbal resolutions of the Social-Democrats, but should have replied by a genuine mass struggle, which would have made the fulfilment of the fascist plans of the German bourgeoisie more difficult.

It should not have allowed the prohibition of the League of Red Front Fighters by the government of Braun and Severing, and should have established fighting contact between the League and the Reichsbanner,* with its nearly one million members, and have compelled Braun and Severing to arm both these organisations in order to resist and smash the fascist bands.

It should have compelled the Social-Democratic leaders who headed the Prussian government to adopt measures of defence against fascism, arrest the fascist leaders, close down their press, confiscate their material resources and the resources of the capitalists who were financing the fascist movement, dissolve the fascist organisations, deprive them of their weapons, and so forth.

Furthermore, it should have secured the re-establishment and extension of all forms of social assistance and the introduction of a moratorium and crisis benefits for the peasants —who were being ruined under the influence of crises—by taxing the banks and the trusts, in this way securing for itself the support of the toiling peasantry.   It was the fault of the Social-Democrats of Germany that this was not done, and that is why fascism *was able* to triumph.

Was it inevitable that the bourgeoisie and the nobility

---

* *Reichsbanner*—" The Flag of the Realm," a Social-Democratic semi-military mass organisation.

should have triumphed in *Spain,* a country where the forces
of proletarian revolt are so advantageously combined with
a peasant struggle?

The Spanish Socialists were in the government from the
first days of the revolution. Did they establish fighting contact between the working class organisations of every political
opinion, including the Communists and the Anarchists, and
did they weld the working class into a united trade union
organisation? Did they demand the confiscation of all the
lands of the landlords, the church and the monasteries, in
favour of the peasants in order to win over the latter to the
side of the revolution? Did they attempt to fight for national
self-determination for the Catalonians and the Basques, and
for the liberation of Morocco? Did they purge the army of
monarchist and fascist elements and prepare it for passing
over to the side of the workers and peasants? Did they dissolve the Civil Guard, so detested by the people, the execu-
tioner of every movement of the people? Did they strike
at the fascist party of Gil Robles and at the might of the
Catholic church? No, they did none of these things. They
rejected the frequent proposals of the Communists for united
action against the offensive of the bourgeois-landlord reaction
and fascism; they passed election laws which enabled the reactionaries to gain a majority in the Cortes (parliament), laws
which penalised popular movements, laws under which the
heroic miners of Asturias are now being tried. They had
peasants who were fighting for land shot by the Civil Guard,
and so on.

This is the way in which the Social-Democrats, by dis-
organising and splitting the ranks of the working class,
cleared the path to power for fascism in Germany, in Austria,
in Spain.

Comrades, fascism *also* triumphed for the reason that the
proletariat found itself isolated from its natural allies. Fascism
triumphed because it was able to win over *large masses of
the peasantry,* owing to the fact that the Social-Democrats,
in the name of the working class, pursued what was in fact
an anti-peasant policy. The peasant saw in power a number
of Social-Democratic governments, which in his eyes were an
embodiment of the power of the working class, but not one
of them put an end to peasant want, none of them gave land
to the peasantry. In Germany, the Social-Democrats did not
touch the landlords; they combated the strikes of the agri-

cultural workers, with the result that long before Hitler came to power the agricultural workers of Germany were abandoning the reformist trade unions and in the majority of cases were going over to the Stahlhelm and to the National-Socialists.

Fascism also triumphed for the reason that it was able to penetrate the ranks of the *youth*, whereas the Social-Democrats diverted the working class youth from the class struggle, while the revolutionary proletariat did not develop the necessary educational work among the youth and did not devote sufficient attention to the struggle for its specific interests and demands. Fascism grasped the very acute need of the youth for militant activity, and enticed a considerable section of the youth into its fighting detachments. The new generation of young men and women have not experienced the horrors of war. They have felt the full weight of the economic crisis, unemployment, and the disintegration of bourgeois democracy. But, seeing no prospects for the future, large numbers of young people have proved to be particularly receptive to fascist demagogy, which depicted for them an alluring future should fascism succeed.

In this connection, we cannot avoid referring also to a number of *mistakes committed by the Communist Parties,* mistakes that hampered our struggle against fascism.

In our ranks there were people who intolerably underrated the fascist danger, a tendency which has not everywhere been overcome to this day. Of this nature was the opinion formerly to be met with in our Parties to the effect that " Germany is not Italy," meaning that fascism may have succeeded in Italy, but that its success in Germany was out of the question, because the latter was an industrially and culturally highly developed country, with forty years of traditions of the working class movement, in which fascism was impossible. Or the kind of opinion which is to be met with nowadays, to the effect that in countries of " classical " bourgeois democracy the soil for fascism does not exist. Such opinions may serve and have served to weaken vigilance with regard to the fascist danger, and to render the mobilisation of the proletariat in the struggle against fascism more difficult.

One might also cite a number of instances in which Communists were caught unawares by the fascist *coup*. Remember Bulgaria, where the leadership of our Party took up a " neutral," but in fact opportunist, position with regard to the

coup d'état of June 9, 1923 : Poland, where, in May, 1926, the
leadership of the Communist Party, making a wrong estimate
of the motive forces of the Polish revolution, did not realise
the fascist nature of Pilsudski's *coup*, and trailed in the rear
of events; Finland, where our Party based itself on a false
conception of slow and gradual fascization and overlooked
the fascist *coup* which was being prepared by the leading
group of the bourgeoisie and which caught the Party and the
working class unawares.

When National-Socialism had already become a menacing
mass movement in Germany, certain comrades, like Heinz
Neumann, who regarded the Brüning government as already
a government of fascist dictatorship, boastfully declared : " If
Hitler's ' Third Empire ' ever comes about, it will only be
one and a half metres underground, and above it will be the
victorious power of the workers."

Our comrades in Germany for a long time failed to reckon
with the wounded national sentiments and indignation of the
masses at the Versailles Treaty ; they treated as of little account
the vacillations of the peasantry and the petty bourgeoisie;
they were late in drawing up their programme of social and
national emancipation, and when they did put it forward they
were unable to adapt it to the concrete demands and the level
of the masses.   They were even unable to popularise it
widely among the masses.

In a number of countries the necessary development of a
mass fight against fascism was replaced by sterile hair splitting as to the nature of fascism " in general " and by a
narrow sectarian attitude in presenting and solving the actual
political problems of the Party.

Comrades, it is not simply because we want to dig up the
past that we speak of the causes of the victory of fascism, that
we point to the historical responsibility of the Social-Democrats for the defeat of the working class, and that we also
point out our own mistakes in the fight against fascism. We
are not historians divorced from living reality ; we, active
fighters of the working class, are obliged to answer the question that is tormenting millions of workers : *Can the victory
of fascism be prevented, and how?*   And we reply to these
millions of workers : Yes, comrades, the road in the way of
fascism can be blocked.   It is quite possible.   It depends on
ourselves—on the workers, the peasants and all the toilers !

Whether the victory of fascism can be prevented depends

in the first place on the militant activity displayed by the working class itself, on whether its forces are welded into a single militant army combating the offensive of capitalism and fascism. Having established its fighting unity, the proletariat would paralyse the influence of fascism over the peasantry, the petty bourgeoisie of the towns, the youth and the intelligentsia, and would be able to neutralise one section and win over another section.

Second, it depends on the existence of a strong revolutionary party, correctly leading the struggle of the toilers against fascism. A party which systematically calls on the workers to retreat in the face of fascism and permits the fascist bourgeoisie to strengthen its positions will inevitably lead the workers to defeat.

Third, it depends on whether a correct policy is pursued by the working class towards the peasantry and the petty-bourgeois masses of the towns. These masses must be taken as they are, and not as we should like to have them. It is only in the process of the struggle that they will overcome their doubts and vacillations. It is only provided we adopt a patient attitude towards their inevitable vacillations, it is only with the political help of the proletariat, that they will be able to rise to a higher level of revolutionary consciousness and activity.

Fourth, it depends on whether the revolutionary proletariat exercises vigilance and takes action at the proper time. It must not allow fascism to catch it unawares, it must not surrender the initiative to fascism, it must inflict decisive blows on the latter before it can gather its forces, it must not allow fascism to consolidate its position, it must repel fascism wherever and whenever it manifests itself, it must not allow fascism to gain new positions—all of which the French proletariat is doing so successfully.

These are the main conditions for preventing the growth of fascism and its accession to power.

Fascism—a Ferocious but Unstable Power

The fascist dictatorship of the bourgeoisie is a ferocious power but an unstable one.

What are the chief causes of the instability of the fascist dictatorship?

While fascism has undertaken to overcome the discord and antagonisms within the bourgeois camp, it is rendering these antagonisms even more acute. Fascism endeavours to establish its political monopoly by violently destroying other political parties. But the existence of the capitalist system, the existence of various classes and the accentuation of class contradictions inevitably tend to undermine and explode the political monopoly of fascism. This is not the case in a Soviet country, where the dictatorship of the proletariat is also realised by a party with a political monopoly, but where this political monopoly accords with the interests of millions of toilers and is increasingly being based on the construction of classless society. In a fascist country the party of the fascists cannot preserve its monopoly for long, because it cannot set itself the aim of abolishing classes and class contradictions. It puts an end to the legal existence of bourgeois parties. But a number of them continue to maintain an illegal existence, while the Communist Party even in conditions of illegality continues to make progress, becomes steeled and tempered and leads the struggle of the proletariat against the fascist dictatorship. Hence, under the blows of class contradictions, the political monopoly of fascism is bound to explode.

Another reason for the instability of the fascist dictatorship is that the contrasts between the anti-capitalist demagogy of fascism and its policy of enriching the monopolist bourgeoisie in the most piratical fashion makes its easier to expose the class nature of fascism and tends to shake and narrow its mass basis.

Furthermore, the success of fascism arouses the profound hatred and indignation of the masses, helps to revolutionise them and provides a powerful stimulus for a united front of the proletariat against fascism.

By conducting a policy of economic nationalism (autarchy) and by seizing the greater portion of the national income for the purposes of preparing for war, fascism undermines the whole economic life of the country and accentuates the economic war between the capitalist states. It lends the conflicts that arise among the bourgeoisie the character of sharp and at times bloody collisions, which undermine the stability of the fascist state power in the eyes of the people. A government which murders its own followers, as was the case in Germany on June 30 of last year, a fascist government against which another section of the fascist bourgeoisie is conducting an armed fight (the National-Socialist *putsch* in Austria and the violent attacks of individual fascist groups on the fascist governments in Poland, Bulgaria, Finland and other countries)—a government of this character cannot for long maintain its authority in the eyes of the broad petty-bourgeois masses.

The working class must be able to take advantage of the antagonisms and conflicts within the bourgeois camp, but it must not cherish the illusion that fascism will exhaust itself of its own accord. Fascism will not collapse automatically. It is only the revolutionary activity of the working class which can help to take advantage of the conflicts which inevitably arise within the bourgeois camp in order to undermine the fascist dictatorship and to overthrow it.

By destroying the relics of bourgeois democracy, by elevating open violence to a system of government, fascism shakes democratic illusions and undermines the authority of the law in the eyes of the toiling masses. This is particularly the case in countries such as, for example, Austria and Spain, where the workers have taken up arms against fascism. In Austria, the heroic struggle of the Schutzbund and the Communists, in spite of their defeat, from the very outset shook the stability of the fascist dictatorship. In Spain, the bourgeoisie did not succeed in placing the fascist muzzle on the toilers. The armed struggles in Austria and Spain have resulted in ever wider masses of the working class coming to realise the necessity for a revolutionary class struggle.

Only such monstrous philistines, such lackeys of the bourgeoisie, as the superannuated theoretician of the Second International, Karl Kautsky, are capable of casting reproaches at the workers, to the effect that they should not have taken up arms in Austria and Spain. What would the working class movement in Austria and Spain look like to-day if the working class of these countries had been guided by the treacherous counsels of the Kautskys? The working class would be experiencing profound demoralisation in its ranks.

" The school of civil war," Lenin says, " does not leave the people unaffected. It is a harsh school, and its complete curriculum *inevitably* includes the victories of the counter-revolution, the debaucheries of enraged reactionaries, savage punishments meted out by the old governments to the rebels, etc. But only downright pedants and mentally decrepit mummies can grieve over the fact that nations are entering this painful school; this school teaches the oppressed classes how to conduct civil war; it teaches how to bring about a victorious revolution; it concentrates in the

masses of present-day slaves that hatred which is always harboured
by the downtrodden, dull, ignorant slaves, and which leads those
slaves who have become conscious of the shame of their slavery
to the greatest historic exploits."*

The success of fascism in Germany has, as we know, been
followed by a new wave of fascist onslaughts, which, in
Austria, led to the provocation by Dollfuss, in Spain to the
new onslaughts of the counter-revolutionaries on the revolutionary conquests of the masses, in Poland to the fascist
reform of the constitution, while in France it spurred the
armed detachments of the fascists to attempt a *coup d'état*
in February, 1934. But this victory, and the frenzy of the
fascist dictatorship, called forth a counter-movement for
a united proletarian front against fascism on an international
scale. The burning of the Reichstag, which served as a
signal for the general attack of fascism on the working class,
the seizure and spoliation of the trade unions and the other
working class organisations, the groans of the tortured anti-
fascists rising from the vaults of the fascist barracks and
concentration camps, are making it clear to the masses what
has been the outcome of the reactionary, disruptive role
played by the German Social-Democratic leaders, who rejected the proposal made by the Communists for a joint
struggle against advancing fascism. They are convincing
the masses of the necessity of amalgamating all the forces
of the working class for the overthrow of fascism.

Hitler's victory also provided a decisive stimulus to the
creation of a united front of the working class against
fascism in France. Hitler's victory not only aroused in the
workers the fear of the fate that befell the German workers,
not only inflamed hatred for the executioners of their German class brothers, but also strengthened in them the determination never in any circumstances to allow in their
country what had happened to the working class in
Germany.

The powerful urge towards the united front in all the
capitalist countries shows that the lessons of defeat have
not been in vain. The working class is beginning to act in
a *new way*. The initiative shown by the Communist Party
in the organisation of the united front and the supreme
self-sacrifice displayed by the Communists, by the revolu-

---

* Lenin, " Inflammable Material in World Politics," *Selected
Works,* Vol. IV, p. 298.

tionary workers in the struggle against fascism have resulted in an unprecedented increase in the prestige of the
Communist International. At the same time, within the
Second International, a profound crisis has been developing, which has manifested itself with particular clarity and
has become particularly accentuated since the bankruptcy
of German Social-Democracy.

The Social-Democratic workers are able to convince
themselves ever more forcibly that fascist Germany, with
all its horrors and barbarities, is in the final analysis *the
result of the Social-Democratic policy of class collaboration
with the bourgeoisie.* These masses are coming ever more
clearly to realise that the path along which the German
Social-Democratic leaders led the proletariat must not again
be traversed. Never has there been such ideological dis-
sension in the camp of the Second International as at the
present time. A process of differentiation is taking place
in all the Social-Democratic parties. Within their ranks
two principal camps are forming : side by side with the
existing camp of reactionary elements, who are trying in
every way to preserve the *bloc* between the Social
Democrats and the bourgeoisie, and who furiously reject
a united front with the Communists, *there is beginning to
form a camp of revolutionary elements who entertain doubts
as to the correctness of the policy of class collaboration
with the bourgeoisie, who are in favour of the creation of
a united front with the Communists and who are increasingly
coming to adopt the position of the revolutionary class
struggle.*

Thus fascism, which appeared as the result of the decline
of the capitalist system, in the long run acts as a factor
of *its further disintegration.* Thus fascism, which has undertaken to bury Marxism, the revolutionary movement of the
working class, is, as a result of the dialectics of life and the
class struggle, itself leading to the further *development of
those forces* which are bound to serve as its grave-diggers,
the grave-diggers of capitalism.

II. UNITED FRONT OF THE WORKING CLASS
AGAINST FASCISM.

Comrades, millions of workers and toilers of the capitalist countries, ask the question : How can fascism be prevented from coming into power and how can fascism be
overthrown after it has been victorious? To this the Communist International replies : *The first thing that must be
done, the thing with which to commence, is to form a united
front, to establish unity of action of the workers in every
factory, in every district, in every region, in every country,
all over the world. Unity of action of the proletariat on
a national and international scale is the mighty weapon which
renders the working class capable not only of successful
defence but also of successful counter-offensive against
fascism, against the class enemy.*

Importance of the United Front.

Is it not clear that joint action by the adherents of the
parties and organisations of the two Internationals, the Communist and the Second International, would facilitate the
repulse by the masses of the fascist onslaught, and would
enhance the political importance of the working class?

Joint action by the parties of both Internationals against
fascism, however, would not be confined to influencing their
present adherents, the Communists and Social-Democrats;
it would also exert a powerful influence on the ranks of the
*Catholic, anarchist and unorganised workers, even on those
who had temporarily become the victims of fascist
demagogy.*

Moreover, a powerful united front of the proletariat would
exert tremendous influence on *all other strata of the toiling
people,* on the peasantry, on the urban petty bourgeoisie,
the intelligentsia. A united front would inspire the wavering groups with faith in the strength of the working class.

But even this is not all. The proletariat of the imperialist
countries has possible allies not only in the toilers of its
own countries, but aso in the *oppressed nations of the
colonies and semi-colonies.* Inasmuch as the proletariat is
split both nationally and internationally, inasmuch as one
of its parts supports the policy of collaboration with the
bourgeoisie, in particular its system of oppression in the

colonies and semi-colonies, this alienates from the working class the oppressed peoples of the colonies and semi-colonies and weakens the world anti-imperialist front. Every step on the road to unity of action, directed towards the support of the struggle for the liberation of the colonial peoples on the part of the proletariat of the imperialist countries, denotes the transformation of the colonies and semi-colonies into one of the most important reserves of the world proletariat.

If finally we take into consideration that international unity of action by the proletariat relies on the *steadily growing strength of a proletarian State, a land of socialism, the Soviet Union,* we see what broad perspectives are revealed by the realisation of united action on the part of the proletariat on a national and international scale. The establishment of unity of action by all sections of the working class, irrespective of their party or organisational affiliation, is necessary *even before the majority of the working class is united in the struggle for the overthrow of capitalism and the victory of the proletarian revolution.*

Is it possible to realise this unity of aciton by the proletariat in the individual countries and throughout the whole world? Yes, it is. And it is possible at this very moment. The Communist International *attaches no conditions to unity of action except one, and that an elementary condition acceptable for all workers, viz., that the unity of action be directed against fascism, against the offensive of capital, against the threat of war, against the class enemy.* This is our condition.

The Chief Arguments of the Opponents of the United Front.

What objections can the opponents of the united front have and how do they voice their objections?

Some say : " To the Communists the slogan of the united front is merely a manœuvre." But if it is a manœuvre, we reply, why don't you expose the " Communist manœuvre " by your honest participation in a united front? We declare frankly : " We want unity of action by the working class, so that the proletariat may grow strong in its struggle against the bourgeoisie, in order that while defending to-day its current interests against attacking capital, against fascism, the proletariat may be in a position to-morrow to create the preliminary conditions for its final emancipation."

" The Communists attack us," say others. But listen, we have repeatedly declared : We shall not attack anyone, neither persons nor organisations nor parties, that stand for the united front of the working class against the class enemy. But at the same time it is our duty, in the interests of the proletariat and its cause, to criticise those persons, those organisations, those parties which impede unity of action by the workers.

" We cannot form a united front with the Communists, since they have a different programme," says a third group. But you yourselves say that your programme differs from the programme of the bourgeois parties, and yet this did not and does not prevent you from entering into coalitions with these parties.

" The bourgeois-democratic parties are better allies against fascism than the Communists," say the opponents of the united front and the advocates of coalition with the bourgeoisie. But what does Germany's experience teach? Did not the Social-Democrats form a *bloc* with those " better " allies? And what were the results?

" If we establish a united front with the Communists, the petty bourgeoisie will take fright at the ' Red danger ' and will desert to the fascists," we hear it said quite frequently. But does the united front represent a threat to the peasants, the petty traders, the artisans, the toiling intellectuals? No, the united front is a threat to the big bourgeoisie, the financial magnates, the *Junkers* and other exploiters, whose regime brings complete ruin to all these strata.

" Social-Democracy is for democracy, the Communists are for dictatorship; therefore we cannot form a united front with the Communists," say some of the Social-Democratic leaders. But are we offering you now a united front for the purpose of proclaiming the dictatorship of the proletariat? We make no such proposal for the time being.

" Let the Communists recognise democracy, let them come out in its defence, then we shall be ready for a united front." To this we reply : We are adherents of Soviet democracy, the democracy of the toilers, the most consistent democracy in the world. But in the capitalist countries we defend and shall continue to defend every inch of bourgeois-democratic liberties which are being attacked by fascism and bourgeois reaction, because the interests of the class struggle of the proletariat so dictate.

" But the tiny Communist Parties do not contribute anything by participating in the united front brought about by the Labour Party," say for instance the Labour leaders of Great Britain. Recall how the Austrian Social-Democratic leaders said the same thing with reference to the small Austrian Communist Party, And what have events shown? It was not the Austrian Social-Democratic Party headed by Otto Bauer and Karl Renner that proved right, but the tiny Austrian Communist Party which at the right moment signalled the fascist danger in Austria and called upon the workers to struggle. For the whole experience of the labour movement has shown that the Communists with all their relative insignificance in numbers are the motive power of the militant activity of the proletariat. Besides this, it must not be forgotten that the Communist Parties of Austria or Great Britain are not only the tens of thousands of workers who are supporters of the Party, but are *parts* of the world Communist movement, are *Sections of the Communist International,* the *leading* party of which is the party of a proletariat which has already achieved victory and rules over one-sixth part of the globe.

" But the united front did not prevent fascism from being victorious in the Saar," is another objection advanced by the opponents of the united front. Strange is the logic of these gentlemen! First they leave no stone unturned to ensure the victory of fascism and then they rejoice with malicious glee because the united front which they entered into only at the last moment did not lead to the victory of the workers.

" If we were to form a united front with the Communists, we should have to withdraw from the coalition, and reactionary and fascist parties would enter the government," say the Social-Democratic leaders holding cabinet posts in various countries. Very well. Was not the German Social-Democratic Party in a coalition government? It was. Was not the Austrian Social-Democratic Party in office? It was. Were not the Spanish Socialists in the same government as the bourgeoisie? They were, too. Did the participation of the Social-Democratic Parties in the bourgeois coalition governments in these countries prevent fascism from attacking the proletariat? It did not. Consequently it is as clear as daylight that participation of Social-Democratic ministers in bourgeois governments *is not* a barrier to fascism.

"The Communists act like dictators, they want to prescribe and dictate everything to us." No. We prescribe nothing and dictate nothing. We only make proposals concerning which we are convinced that if realised they will meet the interests of the toiling people. This is not only the right but the duty of all those acting in the name of the workers. You are afraid of the "dictatorship" of the Communists? Let us jointly submit all proposals to the workers, both yours and ours, jointly discuss them and choose, together with all the workers, those proposals which are most useful to the cause of the working class.

Thus all these arguments against the united front *will not bear the slightest criticism.* They are rather the reservations of the reactionary leaders of Social-Democracy, who prefer their united front with the bourgeoisie to the united front of the proletariat.

No. These reservations will not hold water! The international proletariat has known all the bitterness of tribulation caused by the split in the working class, and becomes more and more convinced that *the united front,* that *unity of action by the proletariat on a national and international scale are both necessary and perfectly possible.*

Content and Forms of the United Front.

What is and ought to be the basic content of the united front at the present stage? The defence of the immediate economic and political interests of the working class, the defence of the working class against fascism, must form the *starting point* and *main content* of the united front in all capitalist countries.

We must not confine ourselves to bare appeals to struggle for the proletarian dictatorship, but must also find and advance those slogans and forms of struggle which arise out of the vital needs of the masses, and are commensurate with their fighting capacity at the given stage of development.

We must point out to the masses what they must do *to-day* to defend themselves against capitalist spoliation and fascist barbarity.

We must strive to establish the widest united front with the aid of joint action by workers' organisations of different trends for the defence of the vital interests of the toiling masses. This means :

First, joint struggle really to shift the burden of the consequences of the crisis on to the shoulders of the ruling classes, the shoulders of the capitalists, landlords—in a word to the shoulders of the rich.

Second, joint struggle against all forms of the fascist offensive, in defence of the gains and the rights of the toilers, against the liquidation of bourgeois-democratic liberties.

Third, joint struggle against the approaching danger of imperialist war, a struggle that will impede the preparations for such a war.

We must indefatigably prepare the working class for a *rapid change in forms and methods of struggle* when there is a change in the situation. As the movement grows and the unity of the working class strengthens, we must go further, and prepare the transition *from the defensive to the offensive against capital,* steering towards the *organisation of a mass political strike.* It must be an absolute condition of such a strike to draw into it the main trade unions of the respective countries.

Communists, of course, cannot and must not for a moment abandon their own *independent work* of Communist education, organisation and mobilisation of the masses. However, for the purpose of ensuring that the workers find the road to unity of action, it is necessary to strive at the same time both for short-term and for long-term agreements providing for *joint action with Social-Democratic Parties, reformist trade unions and other organisations of the toilers* against the class enemies of the proletariat. The chief stress in all this must be laid on developing *mass action* locally, *to be carried out by the local organisations* through local agreements.

While loyally carrying out the conditions of all agreements made with them, we shall mercilessly expose all sabotage of joint action on the part of persons and organisations participating in the united front. To any attempt to wreck the agreements—and such attempts may possibly be made—we shall reply by appealing to the masses while continuing untiringly to struggle for the restoration of the broken unity of action.

It goes without saying that the concrete realisation of the united front will take *various* forms in various countries,

depending upon the condition and character of the workers'
organisations and their political level, upon the concrete
situation in the particular country, upon the changes in progress in the international labour movement, etc.

These forms may include for instance : co-ordinated joint
action of the workers to be agreed upon *from case to case* on
definite occasions, on individual demands or on the basis of
a common platform ; co-ordinated actions at *individual enter-
prises* or by *whole industries*; co-ordinated actions on a *local
regional, national* or *international* scale ; co-ordinated actions
for the organisation of the *economic* struggle of the workers,
carrying out of mass *political* actions, for the organisation of
joint *self-defence* against fascist attacks ; co-ordinated action
in the rendering of *aid to political prisoners and their
families,* in the field of struggle against *social reaction;* joint
actions in the defence of the *interests of the youth* and
women, in the field of *co-operative work, cultural activity,
sports, etc.*

It would be insufficient to content ourselves with the conclusion of a pact providing for joint action and the formation of contact committees consisting of the parties and
organisations participating in the united front, like those
we have in France, for instance. That is only the first
step. The pact is an auxiliary means for realising joint action, but by itself it does not constitute a united front.
A contact commission between the leaders of the Communist
and Socialist parties is necessary to facilitate the carrying
out of joint action, but by itself it is far from adequate for
a real development of the united front, for drawing the
broadest masses into the struggle against fascism.

The Communists and all revolutionary workers must
strive for the formation of elective (and in the countries
of fascist dictatorship—selected from the most authoritative
participants in the united front movement) *non-Party class
bodies of the united front* at the *factories,* among the *unemployed,* in the *working class districts,* among the *small
townsmen* and in the *villages.* Only such bodies will be
able to embrace in the united front movement the vast masses
of unorganised toilers also, will be able to assist in developing the initiative of the masses in the struggle against the
offensive of capital, against fascism and reaction, and on this
basis to create the necessary *broad active rank and file of*

the united front, the training of hundreds and thousands of non-Party Bolsheviks in the capitalist countries.

Joint action of the *organised* workers is the beginning, the foundation. But we must not lose sight of the fact that the unorganised masses constitute the vast majority of workers. Thus, in *France* the number of organised workers —Communists, Socialists, trade union members of various trends—is altogether *about one million,* while the total number of workers is *eleven million.* In *Great Brtiain* there are approximately *five million* members of trade unions and parties of various trends. At the same time the total number of workers is *fourteen million.* In the *United States of America* about *five million workers* are organised, while altogether there are *thirty-eight million* workers in that country. About the same ratio holds good for a number of other countries. In " normal " times this mass in the main does not participate in political life. But now this gigantic mass is getting into motion more and more, is being brought into political life, comes out in the political arena.

The creation of non-Party class bodies is the *best form* for carrying out, extending and strengthening the united front among the rank and file of the broadest masses. These bodies will likewise be the best bulwark against every attempt of the opponents of the united front to disrupt the established unity of action of the working class.

The Anti-Fascist People's Front.

In the mobilisation of the toiling masses for the struggle against fascism, the formation of a *broad people's anti-fascist front* on *the basis of the proletarian united front* is a particularly important task. The success of the entire struggle of the proletariat is closely connected with the establishment of a fighting alliance between the proletariat on the one hand and, on the other hand, the toiling peasantry and the mass of the urban petty bourgeoisie which constitute a majority in the population of even industrially developed countries.

In its agitation, fascism, desirous of winning these masses to its own side, tries to set the toiling masses of the cities and the countryside against the revolutionary proletariat, intimidating the petty bourgeoisie with the bugaboo of the " Red danger." We must *turn the spearpoint in the opposite direction* and show the toiling peasants, artisans and toiling intellectuals whence the real danger threatens. We must *show* them *concretely* who piles the burden of taxes and im-

posts on to the peasant, squeezes usurious interest out of
him, and who, while owning the best lands and enjoying
every form of wealth, drives the peasant and his family from
his plot of land and dooms him to unemployment and
poverty. We must explain concretely, explain patiently and
persistently, who ruins the artisans, the handicraftsmen,
with taxes, imposts, high rents and competition impossible
for them to withstand, who throws into the street and deprives of employment the broad masses of the working intelligentsia.

But this is *not enough*.

The fundamental, the most decisive point in establishing
the anti-fascist people's front is *the resolute action of the
revolutionary proletariat* in defence of the demands of these
strata, particularly of the toiling peasantry, demands in line
with the basic interests of the proletariat, combining in the
process of struggle the demands of the working class with
these demands.

In forming the anti-fascist people's front, a correct approach to those organisations and parties to which a considerable number of the toiling peasantry and the mass of
the urban petty bourgeoisie belong is of great importance.

In the capitalist countries the majority of these parties
and organisations, political as well as economic, are still
under the influence of the bourgeoisie and follow it. The
social composition of these parties and organisations is
heterogeneous. They include big kulaks (rich peasants) side
by side with landless peasants, big business men alongside
of petty shopkeepers, but control is in the hands of the
former, the agents of big capital. This makes it our duty
to *approach* these organisations in *different ways*, taking
into consideration that not infrequently the bulk of the membership does not know anything about the real political
character of its leadership. Under certain conditions, we
can and must bend our efforts to the task of drawing these
parties and organisations or certain sections of them to the
side of the anti-fascist people's front, despite their bourgeois
leadership. Such, for instance, is to-day the situation in
France with the Radical Party, in the United States with
various farmers' organisations, in Poland with the " Stron-
nictwo Ludowe," in Yugoslavia with the Croatian Peasants'
Party, in Bulgaria with the Agrarian League, in Greece
with the Agrarians, etc. But irrespective of whether there

is any chance of attracting these parties and organisations to the side of the people's front, our tactics must *under all circumstances* be directed towards drawing the small peasants, artisans, handicraftsmen, etc., among their members into the anti-fascist people's front.

You see consequently that in this field we must put an end all along the line to what frequently occurs in our practical work—the ignoring of or contemptuous attitude towards the various organisations and parties of the peasants, artisans and urban petty-bourgeois masses.

Cardinal Questions of the United Front in Individual Countries.

There are in every country certain *cardinal questions* which at the present stage are agitating vast masses of the population and around which the struggle for the establishment of the united front must be developed. If these cardinal points, cardinal questions, are properly grasped, it will ensure and accelerate the establishment of the united front.

(a) The United States of America.

Let us take, for example, so important a country in the capitalist world as the *United States of America*. There millions of people have been brought into motion by the crisis. The programme for the recovery of capitalism has collapsed. Vast masses are beginning to abandon the bourgeois parties, and are at present at the crossroads.

Incipient American fascism is endeavouring to direct the disillusionment and discontent of these masses into reactionary fascist channels. It is a peculiarity of the development of American fascism that at the present stage it appears principally in the guise of an opposition to fascism, which it accuses of being an " un-American " tendency imported from abroad. In contradistinction to German fascism, which acts under anti-constitutional slogans, American fascism tries to portray itself as the custodian of the constitution and " American democracy." It does not yet represent a directly menacing force. But if it succeeds in penetrating to the broad masses who have become disillusioned with the old bourgeois parties, it may become a serious menace in the very near future.

And what would the success of fascism in the United States entail? For the toiling masses it would, of course, entail the unrestrained strengthening of the regime of ex-

ploitation and the destruction of the working class movement.
And what would be the international significance of this
success of fascism? As we know, the United States is not
Hungary, or Finland, or Bulgaria, or Latvia. The success
of fascism in the United States would change the whole
international situation quite materially.

Under these circumstances, can the American proletariat
content itself with the organisation of only its class conscious
vanguard, which is prepared to follow the revolutionary
path? No.

It is perfectly obvious that the interests of the American
proletariat demand that all its forces dissociate themselves
from the capitalist parties without delay. It must at the
proper time find ways and suitable forms of preventing
fascism from winning over the broad discontented masses
of the toilers. And here it must be said that under American
conditions the creation of a mass party of toilers, a
" Workers' and Farmers' Party," might serve as such a
suitable form. *Such a party would be a specific form of
the mass people's front in America* that should be set up in
opposition to the parties of the trusts and the banks, and
likewise to growing fascism. Such a party, of course, will
be *neither* Socialist *nor* Communist. But it *will have to be*
an anti-fascist party and *not* an anti-Communist party. The
programme of this party must be directed against the banks,
trusts and monopolies, against the principal enemies of the
people who are gambling on its misfortunes. Such a party
will be equal to its task only if it defends the urgent demands
of the working class, only if it fights for genuine social legislation, for unemployment insurance; only if it fights for
land for the white and black share-croppers and for their
liberation from the burden of debt; only if it works for the
cancellation of the farmers' indebtedness; only if it fights
for the equal status of the Negroes; only if it fights for the
demands of the war veterans, and for the interests of the
members of the liberal professions, the small business men,
the artisans. And so on.

It goes without saying that such a party will fight for
the election of its own candidates to local offices, to the state
legislatures, to the House of Representatives and the Senate.

Our comrades in the United States acted rightly in taking
the initiative for the creation of such a party. But they still
have to take effective measures in order to make the creation

of such a party the cause of the masses themselves. The question of forming a " Workers' and Farmers' Party," and its programme, should be discussed at mass meetings of the people. We should develop the most widespread movement for the creation of such a party, and take the lead in it. In no case must the initiative of organising the party be allowed to pass to elements desirous of utilising the discontent of the masses which have become disillusioned in both the bourgeois parties, Democratic and Republican, in order to create a " third party " in the United States, as an anti-Communist party, a party directed against the revolutionary movement.

(b) *Great Britain.*

In *Great Britain,* as a result of the mass action of the British workers, Mosley's fascist organisation has for the time being been pushed into the background. But we must not close our eyes to the fact that the so-called " National Government " is passing a number of reactionary measures directed against the working class, as a result of which conditions are being created in Great Britain, too, which will make it easy for the bourgeoisie, if necessary, to proceed to a fascist regime. At the present stage, fighting the fascist danger in Great Britain means primarily fighting the " National Government " and its reactionary measures, fighting the offensive of capital, fighting for the demands of the unemployed, fighting against wage reductions and for the repeal of all those laws with the help of which the British bourgeoisie is lowering the standard of living of the masses.

But the growing hatred of the working class for the " National Government " is uniting increasingly large numbers under the slogan of the formation of *a new Labour Government* in Great Britain. Can the Communists ignore this frame of mind of the masses, who still retain faith in a Labour Government? No, comrades. We must find a way of approaching these masses. We tell them openly, as did the Thirteenth Congress of the British Communist Party, that we Communists are in favour of a Soviet government, as the only form of government capable of emancipating the workers from the yoke of capital. But you want a Labour Government? Very well. We have been and are fighting hand in hand with you for the defeat of the " National Government." We are prepared to support your

fight for the formation of a new Labour Government, in
spite of the fact that both the previous Labour Governments
did not fulfil the promises made to the working class by the
Labour Party. We do not expect this government to carry
out Socialist measures. But *we shall present it with the
demand,* in the name of the working class millions, that it
defend the most essential economic and political interests
of the working class and of all toilers. Let us jointly discuss
a common programme of such demands, and let us achieve
that unity of action which the proletariat requires in order
to repel the reactionary offensive of the " National Government," the attack of capital and fascism, and the preparations for a new war. On this basis, the British comrades are
prepared at the forthcoming parliamentary elections to co-
operate with branches of the Labour Party against the
" National Government," and also against Lloyd George,
who is endeavouring in his own way to lure the masses into
following him against the cause of the working class and
in the interests of the British bourgeoisie.

This position of the British Communists is a correct one.
It will help them to set up a militant united front with the
millions of members of the British trade unions and the
British Labour Party.

While always remaining in the front ranks of the fighting
proletariat, and pointing out to the masses the only right
path—the path of the struggle for the revolutionary overthrow of the rule of the bourgeoisie and the establishment of
a Soviet government—the Communists, in defining their
immediate political aims, must not attempt to leap over those
necessary stages of the mass movement in the course of
which the working class masses by their own experience
outlive their illusions and pass over to the side of
Communism.

(c) *France.*

France, as we know, is a country in which the working
class is setting an example to the whole world proletariat of
how to fight fascism. The French Communist Party is
setting an example to all the sections of the Comintern of
how the tactics of the united front should be conducted;
the Socialist workers are setting an example of what the
Social-Democratic workers of other capitalist countries
should now be doing in the fight against fascism. The

significance of the anti-fascist demonstration, attended by half a million people, held in Paris on July 14th of this year, and of the numerous demonstrations in other French cities is tremendous. This is not merely a movement of a united working class front; it is the beginning of a wide general front of the people against fascism in France.

This united front movement enhances the confidence of the working class in its own forces; it strengthens its consciousness of the leading role it is playing in relation to the peasantry, the petty bourgeoisie of the towns and the intelligentsia; it extends the influence of the Communist Party among the working class masses, and therefore brings new strength to the proletariat in the fight against fascism. It is mobilising in good time the vigilance of the masses in regard to the fascist danger. And it will serve as an infectious example for the development of the anti-fascist struggle in other capitalist countries and will exercise a heartening influence on the proletarians of Germany crushed down by the fascist dictatorship.

The victory, needless to say, is a big one, but it still does not decide the issue of the anti-fascist struggle. The overwhelming majority of the French people are undoubtedly opposed to fascism. But the bourgeoisie is able by armed force to violate the will of peoples. The fascist movement is continuing to develop absolutely freely, with the active support of monopoly capital, the State apparatus of the bourgeoisie, the general staff of the French army, and the reactionary leaders of the Catholic church—that stronghold of all reaction. The most powerful fascist organisation, the *Croix de Feu,* now commands 300,000 armed men, the backbone of which consists of 60,000 officers of the reserve. It holds strong positions in the police, the gendarmerie, the army, the air force and in all government offices. The recent municipal elections have shown that in France it is not only the revolutionary forces that are growing, but also the forces of fascism. If fascism succeeds in penetrating widely among the peasantry, and in securing the support of one section of the army, while the other section remains neutral, the French toiling masses will not be able to prevent the fascists from coming to power. Comrades, do not forget the organisational weakness of the French labour movement, which tends to facilitate the success of the fascist attack. The working class and all anti-fascists in France have no grounds for resting content with the results already achieved.

What are the tasks confronting the working class in France?

First, to achieve the establishment of a united front not only in the political sphere, but also in the economic sphere in order to organise the struggle against the capitalist offensive, and by its pressure to smash the resistance offered to the united front by the leaders of the reformist Confederation of Labour.

Second, to achieve trade union unity in France—united trade unions based on the class struggle.

Third, to enlist in the anti-fascist movement the broad peasant masses, the petty-bourgeois masses, devoting special attention in the programme of the anti-fascist people's front to their urgent demands.

Fourth, to strengthen organisationally and extend further the anti-fascist movement which has already developed, by the widespread creation of elected non-Party bodies of the anti-fascist people's front, the influence of which extends to wider masses than those in the parties and toilers' organisations in France at present in existence.

Fifth, to secure by their pressure the disbanding and disarming of the fascist organisations, as organisations of conspirators against the republic and agents of Hitler in France.

Sixth, to achieve the purging of the State apparatus, the army and the police of the conspirators who are preparing a fascist *coup.*

Seventh, to develop the struggle against the leaders of the reactionary cliques of the Catholic church, as one of the most important strongholds of French fascism.

Eighth, to link the army up with the anti-fascist movement by creating in its ranks committees for the defence of the republic and the constitution, directed against those who want to utilise the army for an anti-constitutional *coup d'état;* not to allow the reactionary forces in France to wreck the Franco-Soviet agreement, which defends the cause of peace against the aggression of German fascism.

And if in France the anti-fascist movement leads to the formation of a government which will carry on a real struggle against French fascism—not in word but in deed —will carry out the programme of demands of the anti-fascist people's front, the Communists, *while remaining* the irreconcilable foes of every bourgeois government and supporters of a Soviet government, will nevertheless, in face of the growing fascist danger, *be prepared to support such a government.*

The United Front and the Fascist Mass Organisations.

Comrades, the fight for the establishment of a united front in countries where the fascists are in power is perhaps the most important problem that confronts us. In such countries, of course, the fight is carried on under far more difficult conditions than is the case in countries which have legal labour movements. Nevertheless, all the conditions exist in fascist countries for the development of a real anti-fascist people's front in the struggle against the fascist dictatorship, since the Social-Democratic, Catholic and other workers, in Germany for instance, are in a position to realise more directly the necessity for a joint struggle with the Communists against the fascist dictatorship. Wide strata of the petty bourgeoisie and the peasantry, having already tasted the bitter fruits of fascist rule, are growing increasingly discontented and disillusioned, which fact makes it easier to enlist them in the anti-fascist people's front.

But the principal task in fascist countries, particularly in Germany and Italy, where fascism has managed to gain a mass basis and has forced the workers and other toilers into its organisations, consists in a skilful combination of the struggle against the fascist dictatorship from without and its undermining from within, inside the fascist mass organisations and bodies. Special methods and means of approach suited to the concrete conditions prevailing in these countries must be learned, mastered and applied, so as to facilitate the rapid disintegration of the mass basis of fascism and to prepare the way for the overthrow of the fascist dictatorship. We must learn, master and apply this, and not only shout " Down with Hitler !" and " Down with Mussolini !" Yes, learn, master and apply.

This is a difficult and complex task. It is all the more difficult because our experience in successfully combating the fascist dictatorship is extremely limited. Our Italian comrades, for instance, have already been fighting under the conditions of a fascist dictatorship for about thirteen years. Nevertheless, they have not succeeded in developing a real mass struggle against fascism, and therefore they

have unfortunately been little able in this respect to help
the Communist Parties in other fascist countries by their
positive experience.

The German and Italian Communists, and the Communists in other fascist countries, as well as the Communist
youth, have displayed prodigies of valour; they have made
and are daily making tremendous sacrifices. We all bow
our heads in honour of such heroism and sacrifices. But
heroism alone is not enough. Heroism must be combined
with day-to-day work among the masses, with such concrete
struggle against fascism as will achieve the most tangible
results in this sphere. In our struggle against fascist dictatorship it is particularly dangerous to confuse the wish with
the fact. We must base ourselves on the facts, on the actual
concrete situation.

And what is now the actual situation, in Germany for
instance?

The masses are becoming increasingly discontented and
disillusioned with the policy of the fascist dictatorship, and
this even assumes the form of partial strikes and other acts.
In spite of all its efforts, fascism has failed to win over politically the basic masses of the workers; it is even losing its
former supporters, and will lose them more and more in the
future. Nevertheless, we must realise that the workers who
are convinced *of the possibility* of overthrowing the fascist
dictatorship, and who are prepared, already to-day, to fight
for it actively are still in the minority—they consist of us,
the Communists, and the revolutionary section of the Social-
Democratic workers. But the majority of the toilers have
not yet become aware of the real, concrete possibilities and
methods of overthrowing this dictatorship and are maintaining a waiting position. This we must bear in mind when
we outline our tasks in the struggle against fascism in Germany, and when we seek, study and apply special methods
of bringing about the undermining and overthrow of the
fascist dictatorship in Germany.

In order to be able to strike a telling blow at the fascist
dictatorship, we must first find out what is its most vul-
nerable point. What is the Achilles' heel of the fascist dictatorship? Its social basis. The latter is extremely heterogeneous. It is made up of various classes and various stratas
of society. Fascism has proclaimed itself the sole representa-
tive of all classes and strata of the population: the manu-

facturer and the worker, the millionaire and the unemployed, the *Junker* and the small peasant, the big capitalist and the artisan. It pretends to defend the interests of *all* these strata, the interests of the nation. But since it is a dictatorship of the big bourgeoisie, fascism must inevitably come into conflict with its mass social basis, all the more since, under the fascist dictatorship, the class contradictions between the pack of financial magnates and the overwhelming majority of the people are brought out in greatest relief.

We can lead the masses to a decisive struggle for the overthrow of the fascist dictatorship only by getting the workers who have been forced into the fascist organisations, or have joined them through ignorance, to take part in *the most elementary movements* for the defence of their economic, political and cultural interests. It is for this reason that the Communists must work in these organisations, as the best champions of the day-to-day interests of the mass of members, and must bear in mind that as the workers belonging to these organisations begin more and more frequently to demand their rights and defend their interests, they inevitably come into conflict with the fascist dictatorship.

In defending the urgent and, at first, the most elementary interests of the toiling masses of town and country, it is comparatively easier to find a common language not only with the conscious anti-fascists, but also with those toilers who are still supporters of fascism, but are disillusioned and dissatisfied with its policy, and are grumbling and seeking an occasion for expressing their discontent. We must in general realise that all our tactics in countries where a fascist dictatorship prevails must be of such a character as not to repulse the rank-and-file supporters of fascism, not to throw them once more into the arms of fascism, but to deepen the chasm between the fascist leaders and the mass of disillusioned rank-and-file followers of fascism drawn from the toiling strata.

We need not be dismayed, comrades, if the people mobilised around these day-to-day interests consider themselves either indifferent to politics or even followers of fascism. The important thing for us is to draw them into the movement which although it may not at first proceed openly under the slogans of the struggle against fascism, is already objectively an anti-fascist movement counterposing these masses against the fascist dictatorship.

Experience teaches us that the view that it is *generally impossible,* in countries where a fascist dictatorship prevails, to come out legally or semi-legally, is harmful and incorrect. To insist on this point of view means to fall into passivity, and to renounce real mass work in general altogether, True, under the conditions of a fascist dictatorship, to find forms and methods of legal or semi-legal action is a difficult and complex problem. But, as in many other questions, the path is indicated by life and by the initiative of the masses themselves, which have already provided us with a number of examples that must be generalised and applied in an organised and effective manner. We must very resolutely put an end to the tendency to underestimate work in the fascist mass organisations. In Italy, in Germany and in a number of other fascist countries, our comrades concealed their passivity, and frequently even their direct refusal to work in the fascist mass organisations, by putting work in the factories in contradistinction to work in the fascist mass organisations. In reality, however, it was just this mechanical distinction which led to work being conducted very feebly, and sometimes not at all, both in the fascist mass organisations and in the factories.

Yet it is particularly important that Communists in the fascist countries should be wherever the masses are to be found. Fascism has deprived the workers of their own legal organisations. It has forced the fascist organisations upon them, and it is *there that the masses are* by compulsion, or to some extent voluntarily. These mass fascist organisations can and must be made our legal or semi-legal field of action, where we can meet the masses. They can and must be made our legal or semi-legal starting point for the defence of the day-to-day interests of the masses. In order to utilise these possibilities, Communists must strive to win elective posts in the fascist mass organisations, with the object of establishing contact with the masses, and must rid themselves once and for all of the prejudice that this kind of activity is unseemly and unworthy of a revolutionary worker.

In Germany, for instance, there exists a system known as shop delegates. But where is it stated that we must leave the fascists a monopoly in these organisations? Cannot we endeavour to unite the Communist, Social-Democratic, Catholic and other anti-fascist workers in the factories so that when the list of shop delegates is voted upon the known agents of the employers may be struck off and other candidates, enjoying the confidence of the workers, inserted in their stead? Practice has already shown that this is possible.

And does not practice also go to show that it is possible, jointly with the Social-Democratic and other discontented workers, to demand that the shop delegates really defend the interests of the workers?

Take the " *Labour Front* " in Germany, or the fascist trade unions in Italy. Is it not possible to demand that the functionaries of the " Labour Front " be elected, and not appointed; to insist that the leading bodies of the local groups report to the meetings of the members of the organisations; to address these demands, following a decision by the group, to the employer, to the " guardian of labour," to the higher bodies of the " Labour Front "? This is possible, provided the revolutionary workers really work within the " Labour Front " and try to obtain posts in it.

Similar methods of work are possible and essential in other mass fascist organisations also—in the Hitler Youth Leagues, in the sports organisations, in the *Kraft durch Freude* organisations (*Strength Through Joy*), in the *Doppo Lavoro* in Italy, in the co-operatives, and so forth.

Comrades, you will remember the ancient tale of the capture of Troy. Troy was inaccessible to the armies attacking her thanks to her impregnable walls. And the attacking army, after suffering many sacrifices, was unable to achieve victory until with the aid of the famous Trojan horse it managed to penetrate to the very heart of the enemy's camp.

We revolutionary workers, it appears to me, should not be shy about using the same tactics with regard to our fascist foe, who is defending himself against the people with the help of the living wall of his cutthroats.

He who fails to understand the necessity of applying such tactics in the case of fascism, he who regards such an approach as " humiliating," may be a most excellent comrade, but, if you will allow me to say so, he is a windbag and not a revolutionary, he will be unable to lead the masses to the overthrow of the fascist dictatorship.

Growing up *inside and outside* the fascist organisations in Germany, Italy and the other countries in which fascism possesses a mass basis, the mass movement for a united front, starting with the advocacy of the most elementary requirements, changing its forms and watchwords of the struggle as that struggle extends and grows, will be the *battering ram* that will shatter what now seems to many to be the impregnable fortress of the fascist dictatorship.

The United Front in the Countries where the Social-Democrats are in Office.

The struggle for the establishment of the united front raises also another very important problem, the problem of the united front in countries where Social-Democratic governments, or coalition governments in which Socialists participate, are in power, as, for instance, in Denmark, Norway, Sweden, Czechoslovakia and Belgium.

Our attitude of absolute opposition to Social-Democratic governments, which are governments of compromise with the bourgeoisie, is well known. But this notwithstanding, we do not regard the existence of a *Social-Democratic government* or a coalition government formed by a Social-Democratic party with bourgeois parties as an *insurmountable* obstacle for the establishment of a united front with the Social-Democrats on definite issues. We believe that in such a case also a united front for the defence of the vital interests of the toiling people and in the struggle against fascism is quite *possible* and *necessary*. It stands to reason that in countries where representatives of Social-Demoratic parties take part in the government, the Social-Democratic leadership offers the greatest *resistance* to the proletarian united front. This is quite comprehensible. After all, they want to show the bourgeoisie that it is they who can keep the discontented working classes under control and prevent them from falling under the influence of Communism better and more skilfully than anyone else. The fact, however, that Social-Democratic ministers are opposed to the proletarian united front can by no means justify a situation in which *the Communists do nothing to establish a united front of the proletariat.*

Our comrades in the Scandinavian countries often follow the line of least resistance, *confining themselves to propaganda exposing the Social-Democratic governments.* This is a mistake. In *Denmark,* for example, the Social-Democratic leaders have been in the government for the last ten years and for ten years day in and day out the Communists have been reiterating that it is a bourgeois, a capitalist government. We have to assume that the Danish workers are acquainted with this propaganda. The fact that a considerable majority nevertheless vote for the Social-Democratic government party only goes to show that the exposure of the government on the part of the Communists by means of propaganda *is insufficient*. It does *not* prove, however, that these hundreds of thousands of workers are satisfied with all the government measures of the Social-Democratic ministers. No, they are *not satisfied* with the fact that by its so-called " crisis agreement " the Social-Democratic government assists the *big capitalists and landowners* and not the workers and poor peasants. They are not satisfied with the decree issued by the government in January, 1933, which deprived the workers *of the right to strike*. They are not satisfied with the government decision to *re-arm the police and quarter them in barracks*. They are not satisfied with the project of the Social-Democratic leadership for a dangerous *anti-democratic electoral reform* (which would considerably reduce the number of deputies). I shall hardly be in error, comrades, if I state that 99 per cent. of the Danish workers *do not approve* of these political steps taken by the Social-Democratic leaders and ministers.

Is it not possible for the Communists to call upon the trade union and Social-Democratic organisations of Denmark to discuss the various burning issues, to express their opinions on them and jointly come out for a proletarian united front with the object of obtaining the workers' demands? In October of last year, when our Danish comrades appealed to the trade unions to act against the reduction of unemployment relief and for the democratic rights of the trade unions, about a hundred local trade union organisations joined the united front.

In *Sweden* a Social-Democratic government is for the third time in power, but the Swedish Communists have for a long time refused to apply the united front tactics in practice. Why? Was it because they were opposed to the united front? No, in principle, of course, they were for the united front, for a united front *in general,* but they failed to understand in what circumstances, on what questions, in defence of what demands a proletarian united front could be successfully established. where and how to " hook on." A few months before the Social-Democratic Party formed its government, it advanced during the elections a platform containing demands which were the very thing to include in a platform of the proletarian united front. For example, the slogans " *Against customs duties,*" " *Against militarisation,*" " Make an end to the policy of delay in the question of *unemployment insurance,*" " Grant *adequate old age pensions,*" " *Prohibit organisations like the* ' *Munch* ' *corps* " (a fascist organisation), " Down with *class legislation against the unions* demanded by the bourgeois parties."

Over a million toilers of Sweden voted in 1932 for these demands advocated by the Social-Democrats and welcomed in 1933 the formation of a Social-Democratic government in the hope that now these demands would be realised. What could have been more natural in such a situation and what would have suited the working masses better than an appeal of the Communist Party to all Social-Democratic and trade union organisations to take joint action to *secure these demands advanced by the Social-Democratic Party* ?

If we had succeeded in really mobilising the broad masses, in welding the Social-Democratic and Communist workers' organisations into a united front to secure these demands which the Social-Democrats themselves had advanced, no one can doubt that the *working class of Sweden* would have gained thereby. The Social-Democratic ministers of Sweden, of course, would not have been very happy over it, for in that case the government would have been compelled to meet at least some of these demands. At any rate, what has happened now, when the government instead of abolishing has *raised* some of the duties, instead of restricting militarism has enlarged the military budget, and instead of rejecting any legislation directed against the trade unions has *itself* introduced such a bill in Parliament, would not have happened. True, on the last issue the Communist Party of Sweden carried through a good mass campaign in the spirit of the proletarian united front with the result that in the end even the Social-Democratic parliamentary fraction felt constrained to vote against the government bill, with the result that for the time being the bill has been defeated.

The *Norwegian* Communists were right in calling upon the organisations of the Labour Party to organise joint May Day demonstrations and in putting forward a number of demands which in the main coincided with the demands contained in the election platform of the Norwegian Labour Party. Although this step in favour of a united front was poorly prepared and the leadership of the Norwegian Labour

Party opposed it, *united front demonstrations took place in thirty localities.*

Formerly many Communists used to be afraid that it would be opportunism on their part if they did not counter *every* partial demand of the Social-Democrats by demands of their own which were twice as radical. That was a naive mistake. If Social-Democrats, for instance, demanded the dissolution of the fascist organisations, there was no reason why we should add: " and the disbanding of the State police " (a demand which would be expedient under different circumstances). We should rather tell the Social-Democratic workers : We are ready to accept these demands of your party as demands of the proletarian united front and are ready to fight to the end for their realisation. Let us join hands for the battle.

In *Czechoslovakia* also certain demands advanced by the Czech and the German Social-Democrats, and the reformist trade unions, can and should be utilised for the establishment of a united front of the working class. When the Social-Democrats, for instance, demand work for the unemployed, or the abolition of the laws restricting municipal self-government, as they have done ever since 1927, these demands must be made concrete in each locality, in each district, and a fight must be carried on hand in hand with the Social-Democratic organisations for their actual realisation. Or, when the Social-Democratic parties thunder against the exponents of fascism in the State apparatus " in general," the proper thing to do is in each particular district to drag into the light of day the particular local fascist spokesmen, and together with the Social-Democratic workers demand their removal from government employ.

In *Belgium* the leaders of the Socialist Party, with Emile Vandervelde at their head, have entered a coalition government. This " success " they have achieved thanks to their lengthy and extensive campaign for two main demands : (1) *The abolition of the emergency decrees,* and (2) *The realisation of the de Man plan.* The first issue is very important. The preceding government issued 150 reactionary emergency decrees, which are an extremely heavy burden on the toiling people. It was proposed to repeal them at once. Such was the demand of the Socialist Party. But have many of these emergency decrees been repealed by the new government? It has not rescinded a single one. It has only mollified somewhat a few of the emergency decrees in order to make a sort of " token payment " in settlement of the generous promises of the Belgian Socialist leaders (like that " token dollar " which some European powers proffered the U.S.A. in payment of the millions due as war debts).

As regards the realisation of the widely advertised de Man plan, the matter has taken a turn quite unexpected by the Social-Democratic masses. The Socialist ministers announced that *the economic crisis must be overcome first,* and only those provisions of de Man's plan should be carried into effect which improve the position of the industrial capitalists and the banks; only thereafter would it be possible to adopt measures to improve the conditions of the workers. But *how long* must the workers wait for *their* share in the " benefits " promised them in the de Man plan? The Belgian *bankers* have already had their veritable *shower of gold.* The Belgian franc has been devaluated 28 per cent.; by this manipulation the bankers were able to pocket 4,500,000,000 francs as their spoils at the expense of the wage earners and the savings of the small depositors. But how does this tally with the contents of the de Man plan? Why, if we are to believe the letter of the plan, it promises to " *prosecute* monopolist abuses and speculative manipulations."

On the basis of the de Man plan, the government has appointed a commission to supervise the banks. But the commission *consists of bankers* who can now gaily and light-heartedly supervise themselves.

The de Man plan also promises a number of other good things, such as a " *shortening of the working day,*" " *normalisation of wages,*" " *a minimum wage,*" " organisation of an all-embracing system of *social insurance,*" greater convenience in living conditions through new *housing construction,* and so forth. These are all demands which we Communists can support. We should go to the labour organisations of Belgium and say to them : The capitalists have already received enough and even too much. Let us demand that the Social-Democratic ministers now carry out the promises they made to the workers. Let us get together in a *united front* for the *successful defence* of our interests. Minister Vandervelde, we support the demands on behalf of the workers contained in *your* platform; but we tell you frankly that we take these demands *seriously,* that we want action and not empty words, and therefore are uniting hundreds of thousands of workers *to struggle* for these demands!

Thus, in countries having Social-Democratic governments, the Communists ought to make use of appropriate individual demands taken from the platforms of the Social-Democratic parties themselves, and of the election promises of the Social-Democratic ministers as the starting point for the realisation of joint action with the Social-Democratic parties and organisations, so that they may afterwards the more easily develop a campaign for the establishment of a united front, but on the basis of other mass demands to be raised in the struggle against the offensive of capital, against fascism and the threat of war.

It must further be borne in mind that if in general, joint action with the Social-Democratic parties and organisations requires that the Communists exercise serious and substantiated criticism of Social-Democracy as the ideology and practice of class collaboration with the bourgeoisie, and untiringly explain to the Social-Democratic workers in a comradely way the programme and slogans of Communism, in countries having Social-Democratic governments this task is of particular importance in the struggle for the united front.

The Struggle for Trade Union Unity.

Comrades, the most important stage in the consolidation of the united front must be the establishment of national and international trade union unity.

As you know, the disruptive tactics of the reformist leaders were applied most virulently in the trade unions. The reason for this is clear. Here their policy of class collaboration with the bourgeoisie found its practical culmination directly in the factories, to the detriment of the vital interests of the working class. This, of course, gave rise to sharp criticism and resistance on the part of the revolutionary workers under the leadership of the Communists. That is why the struggle between Communism and reformism raged most fiercely in the trade unions.

The more difficult and complicated the situation became for capitalism, the more reactionary was the policy of the leaders of the Amsterdam unions and the more aggressive were their measures against all opposition elements within the trade unions. Even the establishment of the fascist dictatorship in Germany and the intensified capitalist offensive in all capitalist countries failed to diminish their aggressiveness. Is it not a characteristic fact that in 1933 alone most disgraceful circulars were issued in Holland, Belgium and Sweden urging the expulsion of Communists and revolutionary workers from the trade unions?

The same year a circular was issued in Great Britain prohibiting the local branches of the trade unions from joining anti-war or other revolutionary organisations. That was a prelude to the notorious " black circular " of the Trade Union Congress General Council, which outlawed any trades council admitting delegates " directly or indirectly associated with Communist organisations." What is there left to be said of the leadership of the German trade unions, which applied unprecedented repressive measures against the revolutionary elements in the trade unions?

We must base our tactics, not on the behaviour of individual leaders of the Amsterdam unions, no matter what difficulties their behaviour may cause the class struggle, but primarily on the question of *where the masses of workers are to be found.* And here we must openly declare that work in the trade unions is the sorest spot in the work of all Communist Parties. We must bring about a real change for the better in trade union work and make the question of struggle for trade union unity the central issue.

" What constitutes the strength of Social-Democracy in the West?" asked Comrade Stalin ten years ago. Answering this question, he said :

" The fact that it has its support in the trade unions.

" What constitutes the weakness of our Communist Parties in the West?

" The fact that they are not yet linked with the trade unions, and that certain elements within the Communist Parties do not wish to be linked with them.

" Hence, the main task of the Communist Parties of the West at the present time is to develop the campaign for unity in the trade union movement and to bring it to its consummation; to see to it that all Communists, without exception, join the trade unions, there to work systematically and patiently to strengthen the solidarity of the working class in its fight against capital, and thus attain the conditions that will enable the Communist Parties to rely upon the trade unions."*

Has this precept of Comrade Stalin's been followed? No, comrades, it has not.

Ignoring the urge of the workers to join the trade unions, and faced with the difficulties of working within the Amster-

---

* Stalin, " The Results of the Work of the Fourteenth Conference of the R.C.P.," *Leninism,* Vol. I, p. 160.

dam unions, many of our comrades decided to pass by this complicated task. They invariably spoke of an organisational crisis in the Amsterdam unions, of the workers deserting the unions, but failed to notice that after some decline at the beginning of the world economic crisis, these unions later began to grow again. The peculiarity of the trade union movement has been precisely the fact that the attacks of the bourgeoisie on trade union rights, the attempts in a number of countries to unify the trade unions (Poland, Hungary, etc.), the curtailment of social insurance, and wage cuts, forced the workers notwithstanding the lack of resistance displayed by the reformist trade union leaders to rally still more closely around these unions, because the workers wanted and still want to see in the trade unions the militant champions of their vital class interests. This explains the fact that most of the Amsterdam unions in France, Czechoslovakia, Belgium, Holland, Sweden, Switzerland, etc., have grown in membership during the last few years. The American Federation of Labour has also considerably increased its membership in the past two years.

Had the German comrades better understood the problem of trade union work of which Comrade *Thälmann* spoke on many occasions, we would undoubtedly have had a better situation in the trade unions than was the case at the time the fascist dictatorship was established. By the end of 1932 only about *ten per cent.* of the Party members belonged to the free trade unions. This in spite of the fact that after the Sixth Congress of the Comintern the Communists took the lead in quite a number of strikes. Our comrades used to write in the press of the need to assign 90 per cent. of our forces to work in the trade unions, but in reality activity was concentrated exclusively around the revolutionary trade union opposition which actually sought to replace the trade unions. And how about the period after Hitler's seizure of power? For two years many of our comrades stubbornly and systematically opposed the correct slogan of fighting for the re-establishment of the free unions.

I could cite similar examples about almost every other capitalist country.

But we already have the first serious achievements to our credit in the struggle for trade union unity in European countries. I have in mind little Austria, where on the initiative of the Communist Party a basis has been created for

an illegal trade union movement. After the February
battles the Social-Democrats, with Otto Bauer at the head,
threw out the watchword : " The free unions can be re-
established only after the downfall of fascism." The Communists applied themselves to the *task of re-establishing the
trade unions.* Each phase of that work was a bit of the
living united front of the Austrian proletariat. The successful re-establishment of the free trade unions in underground
conditions was a serious blow to fascism. The Social-
Democrats were at the parting of the ways. Some of them
tried to negotiate with the government. Others, seeing our
successes, created their own parallel illegal trade unions.
But there could be only one road : *either capitulation to
fascism, or towards trade union unity through joint struggle
against fascism.* Under mass pressure, the wavering leadership of the parallel unions created by the former trade union
leaders decided to agree to amalgamation. The basis of
this amalgamation is irreconcilable struggle against the
offensive of capitalism and fascism and the guarantee of
trade union democracy. We welcome this fact of the amalgamation of trade unions, which is the first of its kind since
the formal split of the trade unions after the war and is,
therefore, of *international importance.*

In *France* the united front has unquestionably served as
a mighty impetus towards the establishment of trade union
unity. The leaders of the General Confederation of Labour
have hampered and still hamper in every way the realisation
of unity, countering the main issue of the class policy of
the trade unions by raising issues of a subordinate and secon-
dary or formal character. An unquestionable success in the
struggle for trade union unity has been the establishment of
single unions on a local scale, embracing, in the case of the
railroad workers, for instance, approximately three-quarters
of the membership of both trade unions.

We are definitely for the re-establishment of *trade union
unity in each country and on an international scale. We are
for one union in each industry.*

*We stand for one federation of trade unions in each coun-
try. We are for one international federation of trade unions
organised according to industries.*

*We stand for one International of trade unions based on
the class struggle. We are for united class trade unions as
one of the major bulwarks of the working class against the*

offensive of capital and fascism. Our only condition for uniting the trade unions is: *Struggle against capital, struggle against fascism, and internal trade union democracy.*

Time does not stand still. To us the question of trade union unity on a national as well as international scale is a question of the great task of uniting our class in mighty, single trade union organisations against the class enemy.

We welcome the fact that on the eve of May First of this year the Red International of Labour Unions addressed a letter to the Amsterdam International with the proposal to consider jointly the question of the terms, methods and forms of unification of the world trade union movement. The leaders of the Amsterdam International rejected that proposal, using the stock argument that unity in the trade union movement is possible only within the Amsterdam International, which, by the way, includes almost none but trade unions in European countries.

But the Communists working in the trade unions must continue to struggle indefatigably for the unity of the trade union movement. The task of the Red trade unions and the R.I.L.U. is to do all in their power to hasten the hour of joint struggle of all trade unions against the offensive of capital and fascism, to establish a united trade union movement, despite the stubborn resistance of the reactionary leaders of the Amsterdam International. The Red trade unions and the R.I.L.U. must receive our unstinted support in this matter.

In countries where small Red trade unions exist we recommend them to work for their affiliation with the big reformist unions, but to insist on the right to defend their views and on the reinstatement of expelled members. But in countries where big Red trade unions exist parallel with big reformist trade unions, we must work for the convening of *unity congresses* on the basis of platforms of struggle against the capitalist offensive and of ensuring *trade union democracy.*

It should be stated categorically that any Communist worker, any revolutionary worker who does not belong to the mass trade union of his industry, who does not fight to transform the reformist trade union into a real class trade union organisation, who does not fight for trade union unity on the basis of the class struggle, such a Communist worker, such a revolutionary worker, does not discharge his elementary proletarian duty.

The United Front and the Youth.

I have already pointed out the role which the drawing of the youth into the fascist organisations played in the victory of fascism. In speaking of the youth, we must state frankly that we have neglected our task of drawing the masses of the working youth into the struggle against the offensive of capital, against fascism and the danger of war; we have neglected these tasks in a number of countries. We have underestimated the enormous importance of the youth in the fight against fascism. We have not always taken account of the specific economic, political and cultural interests of the youth. We have likewise not paid proper attention to revolutionary education of the youth.

All this has been utilised very cleverly by fascism, which in some countries, particularly in Germany, has inveigled large sections of the youth on to the anti-proletarian road. It should be borne in mind that the glamour of militarism is not the only enticement with which fascism captures the youth. It feeds and clothes some of them in its detachments, gives work to others, even sets up so-called cultural institutions for the youth, trying in this way to imbue them with the idea that it really can and wants to feed, clothe, teach and provide work for the masses of the toiling youth.

In a number of capitalist countries, our *Young Communist Leagues* are still largely sectarian organisations divorced from the masses. Their fundamental weakness is that they are still trying to copy the Communist Parties, their forms and methods of work, forgetting that the Y.C.L. is *not a Communist Party of the youth*. They do not sufficiently take into consideration the fact that this is an organisation having its own specific tasks. Its methods and forms of work, of education and of struggle, must be adapted to the specific level and needs of the youth.

Our Young Communists have given memorable examples of heroism in the fight against fascist violence and bourgeois reaction. But they still lack the ability to win the masses of the youth away from hostile influences by dint of stubborn, concrete work. This is attested by the fact that they have not yet overcome their opposition to work in the fascist mass organisations, and that their approach

to the Socialist youth and other non-Communist youth is
not always correct.

A great part of the responsibility for all this must be
borne, of course, by the Communist Parties as well, for they
ought to lead and support the Y.C.L. in its work. For the
problem of the youth is not only a Y.C.L. problem. *It is a
problem for the entire Communist movement.* In the struggle
for the youth, the Communist Parties and the Y.C.L.
organisations must actually effect a decisive change. The
main task of the Communist youth movement in capitalist
countries is to advance boldly in the direction of bringing
about the *united front,* along the path of organising and
uniting the toilers of the young generation. The tremendous
importance for the revolutionary movement of the youth
that attaches to even the first steps taken in this direction
is shown by the examples of *France* and the *United States*
during the recent past. It was sufficient in these countries
to proceed to apply the united front, when considerable successes were at once achieved. In the sphere of the international united front, the successful initiative of the anti-
fascist and anti-war committee in Paris in bringing about
the international co-operation of all *non-fascist* youth organisations is also worthy of note in this connection.

These recent successful steps in the united front movement of the youth also show that the forms which the united
front of the youth is to assume must not be stereotyped, nor
be necessarily the same as those met with in the practice
of the Communist Parties. The Young Communist Leagues
must strive in every way to unite the forces of all non-fascist
mass organisations of the youth, including the formation of
various kinds of common organisations for the struggle
against fascism, against the unprecedented manner in which
the youth is being stripped of every right, against the militarisation of the youth and for the economic and cultural
rights of the young generation, in order to draw these young
toilers over to the side of the anti-fascist front, no matter
where they may be—in the factories, the forced labour
camps, the labour exchanges, the army barracks and the
fleet, the schools, or in the various sports, cultural or other
organisations.

In developing and strengthening the Y.C.L., our Y.C.L.
members must work for the formation of anti-fascist asso-

ciations of the Communist and Socialist Youth Leagues on a
platform of class struggle.

Women and the United Front.

Nor was work among toiling women—among working
women, unemployed women, peasant women and house-
wives—underestimated any less than was work among the
youth. While fascism exacts most from youth, it enslaves
women with particular ruthlessness and cynicism, playing
on the most painful feelings of the mother, the housewife,
the single working woman, uncertain of the morrow.
Fascism, posing as a benefactor, throws the starving family
a few beggarly scraps, trying in this way to stifle the bitterness aroused, particularly among the toiling women, by
the unprecedented slavery which fascism brings them. It
drives working women out of industry, forcibly ships needy
girls to the country, reducing them to the position of unpaid
servants of rich farmers and landlords. While promising
women a happy home and family life, it drives women to
prostitution like no other capitalist regime.

Communists, above all our women Communists, must
remember that there cannot be a successful fight against
fascism and war unless the broad masses of women are
drawn into it. And agitation alone will not accomplish this.
We must find a way of mobilising the masses of toiling
women around their vital interests and demands, taking
into account the concrete situation in each instance, in the
fight for their demands against high prices, for higher wages
on the basis of the principle of equal pay for equal work,
against mass dismissals, aganist every manifestation of in-
equality in the status of women, and against fascist enslavement.

In endeavouring to draw the toiling women into the
revolutionary movement, we must not be afraid of forming
separate women's organisations for this purpose, wherever
necessary. The preconceived notion that the women's organisations under Communist Party leadership in the
capitalist countries must be liquidated, as part of the struggle
against " women's separatism " in the labour movement,
has frequently caused a great deal of harm.

It is necessary to seek out the simplest and most flexible
forms, in order to establish contact and bring about co-
operation in struggle between the revolutionary, Social-
Democratic and progressive anti-war and anti-fascist

women's organisations. We must spare no pains to see that
the women workers and toilers fight shoulder to shoulder
with their class brothers in the ranks of the united working
class front and the anti-fascist people's front.

The Anti-Imperialist United Front.

In connection with the changed international and internal
situation, exceptional importance attaches in all colonial and
semi-colonial countries to the question of the *anti-imperialist
united front.*

In forming a wide anti-imperialist united front of struggle
in the colonies and semi-colonies, it is necessary above all
to recognise the variety of conditions in which the anti-
imperialist struggle of the masses is proceeding, the varying
degree of maturity of the national liberation movement, the
role of the proletariat within it and the influence of the
Communist Party over the broad masses.

In Brazil the problem is different from that in India,
China, etc.

In *Brazil* the Communist Party, having laid a correct
foundation for the development of the united anti-imperialist
front by the establishment of the National Liberation
Alliance, has to make every effort to extend further this front
by drawing into it first and foremost the many millions of the
peasantry, leading up to the formation of units of a people's
revolutionary army, completely devoted to the revolution,
and to the establishment of the rule of the National Liberation Alliance.

In *India* the Communists have to support, extend and
participate in anti-imperialist mass activities, not excluding
those which are under national reformist leadership. While
maintaining their political and organisational independence,
they must carry on active work inside the organisations
which take part in the Indian National Congress, facilitating
the process of crystallisation of a national revolutionary
wing among them, for the purpose of further developing
the national liberation movement of the Indian peoples
against British imperialism.

In *China,* where the people's movement has already led
to the formation of Soviet districts over a considerable territory of the country and to the organisation of a powerful
Red Army, the predatory attack of Japanese imperialism
and the treason of the Nanking Government have brought
into jeopardy the national existence of the great Chinese

people. Only the Chinese Soviets can act as a unifying
centre in the struggle against the enslavement and partition
of China by the imperialists, as a unifying centre which
will rally all anti-imperialist forces for the national defence
of the Chinese people.

We therefore approve the initiative taken by our courageous brother Party of China in the creation of a most extensive anti-imperialist united front against Japanese imperialism and its Chinese agents, jointly with all those
organised forces existing on the territory of China which are
ready to wage a real struggle for the salvation of their
country and their people. I am sure that I express the
sentiments and thoughts of our entire Congress if I state
that we send our warmest fraternal greetings, in the name
of the revolutionary proletariat of the whole world, to all
the Soviets of China, to the Chinese revolutionary people.
We send our ardent fraternal greetings to the heroic Red
Army of China, tried in a thousand battles. And we assure
the Chinese people of our firm resolve to support its struggle
for its complete liberation from all imperialist robbers and
their Chinese henchmen.

The Government of the United Front.

Comrades, we have taken a bold and determined course
towards the united front of the working class, and are ready
to carry it out with full consistency.

If we Communists are asked whether we advocate the
united front *only* in the struggle for partial demands, or
whether we are prepared to share the responsibility even when
it will be a question of forming a *government* on the basis of
the united front, then we say with a full sense of our responsibility : Yes, we recognise that a situation may arise in which
the formation of a *government of the proletarian united front,*
or of the *anti-fascist people's front,* will become not only possible but necessary in the interests of the proletariat. And in
that case we shall declare for the formation of such a government without the slightest hesitation.

I am not speaking of a government which may be formed
after the victory of the proletarian revolution. It is not impossible, of course, that in some country, immediately after
the revolutionary overthrow of the bourgeoisie, there may be
formed a Soviet government on the basis of a government
bloc of the Communist Party with a definite party (or its
Left wing) participating in the revolution. After the October

Revolution the victorious Party of the Russian Bolsheviks, as we know, included representatives of the Left Socialist-Revolutionaries in the Soviet government. This was a specific feature of the first Soviet government after the victory of the October Revolution.

I am not speaking of such a case, but of the possible formation of a united front government on the eve of and before the victory of the Soviet revolution.

What kind of government is this? And in what situation could there be any question of such a government?

It is primarily a *government of struggle against fascism and reaction.* It must be a government arising as the result of the united front movement and in no way restricting the activity of the Communist Party and the mass organisations of the working class, but on the contrary taking determined measures against the counter-revolutionary financial magnates and their fascist agents.

At a suitable moment, relying on the growing united front movement, the Communist Party of a given country will declare for the formation of such a government on the basis of a definite anti-fascist platform.

Under what objective conditions will it be possible to form such a government? In the most general terms, our reply to this question will be as follows: Under conditions of *political crisis,* when the ruling classes are no longer in a condition to cope with the mighty upsurge of the mass anti-fascist movement. But this is only a general perspective, without which it is scarcely possible in practice to form a united front government. Only the existence of definite and *specific prerequisites* can put on the order of the day the question of forming such a government as a politically *necessary* task. It seems to me that the following prerequisites deserve the greatest attention in this connection.

First, the state apparatus of the bourgeoisie must already be sufficiently *disorganised* and *paralysed,* so that the bourgeoisie cannot prevent the formation of a government of struggle against reaction and fascism;

Second, the broadest masses of toilers, particularly the mass trade unions, must be in a violent state of revolt *against fascism and reaction, but are not yet ready* to rise in insurrection, to *fight under Communist Party leadership for the achievement of Soviet power;*

Third, the differentiation and Leftward movement in the

ranks of Social-Democracy and other parties participating in
the united front must already have reached the point where a
considerable proportion of them demand *ruthless measures
against the fascists and the other reactionaries*, struggle together with the Communists against fascism, and openly come
out against that reactionary section of their own party which
is hostile to Communism.

When and in what countries a situation will actually arise
in which these prerequisites will be present in a sufficient
degree, it is impossible to state in advance. But inasmuch as
such a possibility *is not precluded in any of the capitalist countries* we must reckon with it, and not only orientate and prepare ourselves but orientate also the working class
accordingly.

The fact that we are bringing up this question for discussion at all to-day is, of course, connected with our evaluation
of the situation and the immediate prospects, also with the
actual growth of the united front movement in a number of
countries during the recent past. For more than ten years
the situation in the capitalist countries has been such that it
was not necessary for the Communist International to discuss
a question of this kind.

You remember, comrades, that at our Fourth Congress,
in 1922, and again at the Fifth Congress, in 1924, the question
of the slogan of a *workers'*, or a *workers' and peasants'
government,* was under discussion. Originally the issue
turned essentially upon a question which was almost
analogous to the one we are discussing to-day. The debates
that took place at that time in the Communist International
concerning this question, and in particular the political *errors*
which were committed in connection with it, have to this day
retained their importance for *sharpening our vigilance against
the danger of deviations to the Right or " Left " from the
Bolshevik line on this question.* Therefore I shall briefly
point out a few of these errors, in order to draw from them the
lessons necessary for the present policy of our Parties.

The *first* series of mistakes was determined precisely by
the circumstance that the question of a workers' government
was not clearly and firmly interlinked with the existence of a
political crisis. Owing to this the *Right opportunists* were
able to interpret matters as though we should strive for the
formation of a workers' government, supported by the Communist Party, in any, so to speak, " normal " situation. The

ultra-Lefts, on the other hand, recognised only such a workers' government as could be formed exclusively by armed insurrection, *after* the overthrow of the bourgeoisie. Both views were wrong. In order to avoid a repetition of such mistakes, we now lay *such great stress on the exact consideration* of the specific, concrete circumstances of the political crisis and the upsurge of the mass movement, in which the formation of a united front government may prove possible and politically necessary.

The *second* series of errors were determined by the circumstance that the question of a workers' government was not interlinked with the development of the militant mass *united front movement of the proletariat.* Thus the *Right opportunists* were enabled to distort the question, reducing it to the unprincipled tactics of forming *blocs* with Social-Democratic Parties on the basis of purely parliamentary arrangements. The *ultra-Lefts,* on the other hand, shouted : " No coalitions with the counter-revolutionary Social-Democrats !" regarding all Social-Democrats as counter-revolutionaries at bottom.

Both were wrong, and we now emphasise, on the one hand, that we are not in the least anxious for such a " workers' government " as would be nothing more or less than an enlarged Social-Democratic government. We even prefer to waive calling it a " workers' government," and *speak of a united front government* which in political character is something absolutely *different, different in principle,* from all the Social-Democratic governments which usually call themselves " workers' (or Labour) governments." While the Social-Democratic government is an instrument of class collaboration with the bourgeoisie in the interest of the preservation of capitalist order, a *united front government* is an instrument of collaboration between the revolutionary vanguard of the proletariat and other anti-fascist parties, in the interest of the entire toiling population, a government of struggle against fascism and reaction. Obviously there is a radical *difference* between these two things.

On the other hand, we emphasise the necessity of seeing *the difference between the two different camps of Social-Democracy.* As I have already pointed out, there is a reactionary camp of Social-Democracy, but alongside of it there exists and is growing the camp of the Left Social-Democrats (without quotation marks), of workers who are becoming revolutionary. The decisive difference between them in practice consists in their attitude to the united front of the working class. The reactionary Social-Democrats are *against* the united front, they slander the united front movement, they sabotage and disintegrate it, as it undermines their policy of compromise with the bourgeoisie. The Left Social-Democrats are *for the united front;* they defend, develop and strengthen the united front movement. Inasmuch as this united front movement is a militant movement against fascism and reaction, it will be a constant motive force, impelling the united front government to struggle against the reactionary bourgeoisie. The more powerfully this mass movement develops, the greater the force which it can offer to the government to combat the reactionaries. And the better this mass movement will be organised *from below,* the wider the network of *non-Party class organs of the united front in the factories,* among the *unemployed,* among the *workers' districts,* among the *small people of town and country,* the greater will be the guarantee against a possible degeneration of the policy of the united front government.

The *third* series of mistaken views which came to light during our former debates touched precisely on the *practical policy* of the " workers' government." The *Right opportunists* considered that a " workers' government " ought to keep " within the framework of bourgeois democracy," and consequently ought not to take any steps going beyond this framework. The *ultra-Lefts,* on the other hand, actually refused to make any attempt to form a united front government.

In 1923 *Saxony* and *Thuringia* presented a clear picture of a Right opportunist " workers' government " in action. The entry of the Communists into the Saxony government jointly with the Left Social-Democrats (Zeigner group) was no mistake in itself ; on the contrary, the revolutionary situation in Germany fully justified this step. But when participating in the government, the Communists should have used their positions primarily *for the purpose of arming the proletariat.* This they did not do. They did not even requisition a single apartment of the rich, although the housing shortage among the workers was so great that many of them were still without a roof over their heads, together with their wives and children. They also did *nothing* to organise the revolutionary mass movement of the workers. They behaved generally like *ordinary* parliamentary ministers

" within the framework of bourgeois democracy." As you know this was the result of the opportunist policy of Brandler and his adherents. The result was such bankruptcy that we are still compelled to refer to the government of Saxony as the classical example of how revolutionaries should *not* behave when in office.

Comrades, we demand of every united front government an entirely different policy. We demand that such a government carry out definite and *fundamental revolutionary demands* required by the situation. For instance, control of production, control of the banks, disbanding of the police, its replacement by an armed workers' militia, etc.

Fifteen years ago Lenin called upon us to focus all our attention on " searching out forms of *transition* or *approach* to the proletarian revolution." It may be that in a number of countries the *united front government* will prove to be *one* of the most important transitional forms. The " Left " doctrinaires always evaded this precept of Lenin's. Like the limited propagandists that they were, they spoke only of " aims," without ever worrying about " forms of transition." The Right opportunists, on the other hand, tried to establish a special " *democratic intermediate stage* " lying between the dictatorship of the bourgeoisie and the dictatorship of the proletariat, for the purpose of instilling into the workers the illusion of a peaceful parliamentary procession from the one dictatorship to the other. This fictitious " intermediate stage " they also called the " transitional form," and even quoted Lenin on the subject! But this piece of swindling was not difficult to expose; for Lenin spoke of the form of transition and approach to the " *proletarian revolution*," i.e., to the overthrow of the bourgeois dictatorship, and *not* of some transitional form *between* the bourgeois and the proletarian dictatorship.

Why did Lenin attribute such exceptionally great importance to the form of transition to the proletarian revolution? Because he bore in mind " *the fundamental law of all great revolutions*," the law that for the masses propaganda and agitation alone cannot take the place of *their own political experience*, when it is a question of attracting really broad masses of the toilers to the side of the revolutionary vanguard, without which a victorious struggle for power is impossible. It is a common mistake of a Leftist character to imagine that as soon as a political (or revolutionary) crisis arises, it is enough for the Communist leaders to throw out the slogan of revolutionary insurrection, and the broad masses will follow them. No, even in such a crisis the masses are far from always being ready to do so. We saw this in the case of *Spain*. To help the *millions* to master as rapidly as possible, through their own experience, what they have to do, where to find a radical solution, what party is worthy of their confidence—these among others are the purposes for which both transitional slogans and special " forms of transition or approach to the proletarian revolution " are necessary. Otherwise the great mass of the people, a prey to petty-bourgeois democratic illusions and traditions, may waver even when there is a revolutionary situation, may procrastinate and stray, without finding the road to revolution and then come under the axe of the fascist executioners.

That is why we indicate the possibility of forming a government of the anti-fascist united front in the conditions of a political crisis. In so far as such a government will really prosecute the struggle against the enemies of the people, and give a free hand to the working class and the Communist Party, we Communists shall accord it our unstinted support, and as soldiers of the revolution shall take our place in the *first line of fire*. But we state frankly to the masses :

Final salvation this government *cannot* bring. It is not in a position to overthrow the class rule of the exploiters, and for this reason cannot finally eliminate the danger of fascist counter-revolution. Consequently it is necessary *to prepare for the socialist revolution!* Soviet power and *only* Soviet power can bring such salvation !

In estimating the present development of the world situation, we see that a *political crisis* is maturing in quite a number of countries. This determines the great urgency and importance of a firm decision by our Congress on the question of a united front government.

If our Parties are able to utilise in a Bolshevik fashion the opportunity of forming a united front government, of waging the struggle for its formation and the existence in power of such a government *for the revolutionary training of the masses,* this will be *the best political justification* of our policy of the formation of united front governments.

The Ideological Struggle Against Fascism.

One of the weakest aspects of the anti-fascist struggle of our Parties lies in the fact that they *react inadequately and too slowly to the demagogy of fascism,* and to this day continue to look with disdain upon the problems of the struggle against fascist ideology. Many comrades did not believe that so reactionary a variety of bourgeois ideology as the ideology of fascism, which in its stupidity frequently reaches the point of lunacy, was capable of gaining a mass influence at all. This was a great mistake. The putrefaction of capitalism penetrates to the innermost core of its ideology and culture, while the desperate situation of the broad masses of the people renders certain sections of them susceptible to infection from the ideological refuse of this putrefaction.

We must under no circumstances underrate this fascist capacity for ideological infection. On the contrary, we must develop for our part an extensive ideological struggle on the basis of clear, popular argument and a correct, well thought-out approach to the peculiarities of the national psychology of the masses of the people.

The fascists are rummaging through the entire *history* of every nation so as to be able to pose as the heirs and continuers of all that was exalted and heroic in its past, while all that was degrading or offensive to the national sentiments of the people they make use of as weapons against the enemies of fascism. Hundreds of books are being published in Germany which pursue only one aim—to falsify the history of the German people and give it a fascist complexion.

The new-baked National-Socialist historians try to depict the history of Germany as if for the last two thousand years, by virtue of some " historical law," a certain line of development had run through it like a red thread which led to the appearance on the historical scene of a national " saviour," a " Messiah," of the *German* people, a certain " corporal " of *Austrian* extraction ! In these books the greatest figures of the German people in the past are represented as having been fascists, while the great peasant movements are set down as the direct precursors of the fascist movement.

Mussolini makes every effort to capitalise the heroic figure of Garibaldi. The French fascists bring to the fore as their heroine Joan of Arc. The American fascists appeal to the traditions of the American War of Independence, the traditions of Washington and Lincoln. The Bulgarian fascists make use of the national liberation movement of the seventies and its heroes beloved of the people, Vassil Levsky, Stephan Karaj, and others.

Communists who suppose that all this has nothing to do with the cause of the working class, who do nothing to enlighten the masses on the past of their own people, in a historically correct fashion, in a genuinely Marxist, a Leninist-Marxist, a Leninist-Stalinist spirit, who do nothing to *link up their present struggle with its revolutionary traditions and past*—voluntarily relinquish to the fascist falsifiers all that is valuable in the historical past of the nation, in order **that the fascists may** bamboozle the masses.

No, comrades, *we are concerned with every important question, not only of the present and the future, but also of the past of our own peoples.* For we Communists do not pursue a narrow policy based on the craft interests of the workers. We are not of those narrow-minded functionaries of the trade unions or leaders of the medieval guild handicraftsmen and journeymen. We are the representatives of the class interests of the most important, the greatest class of modern society—the working class, to whose destiny it falls to free mankind from the sufferings of the capitalist system, the class which on one-sixth of the world has already cast off the yoke of capitalism and constitutes the ruling class. We defend the vital interests of all the exploited toiling strata, *i.e.,* of the overwhelming majority of the people in any capitalist country.

We Communists are the *irreconcilable opponents, on principle,* of bourgeois nationalism of every variety. But we *are not supporters of national nihilism,* and should never act as such. The task of educating the workers and all toilers in the spirit of proletarian internationalism is one of the fundamental tasks of every Communist Party. But whoever thinks that this permits him, or even compels him, to sneer at all the national sentiments of the broad toiling masses is far from genuine Bolshevism, and has understood nothing of the teaching of Lenin and Stalin on the national question.

Lenin, who always fought bourgeois nationalism resolutely and consistently, gave us an example of the correct approach to the problem of national sentiments, in his article " On the National Pride of the Great-Russians," written in 1914. I shall quote a passage :

" Are we enlightened Great-Russian proletarians impervious to the feeling of national pride? Certainly not ! We love our language and our motherland; we, more than any other group, are working to raise *its* labouring masses (*i.e.,* nine-tenths of *its* population) to the level of intelligent democrats and Socialists.

We, more than anybody, are grieved to see and feel to what violence, oppression and mockery our beautiful motherland is being subjected by the tsarist hangmen, the nobles and the capitalists. We are proud of the fact that those acts of violence met with resistance in our midst, in the midst of the Great-Russians; that *we* have given the world Radishchev, the Decembrists, the declassed revolutionaries of the seventies; that in 1905 the Great-Russian working class created a powerful revolutionary party of the masses . . . . We are filled with national pride because of the knowledge that the Great-Russian nation, *too,* has created a revolutionary class; that it, *too,* has proven capable of giving humanity great examples of struggle for freedom and for Socialism; that its contribution is not confined solely to great pogroms, numerous scaffolds, torture chambers, great famines, and great servility before the priests, the tsars, the landowners and the capitalists.

" We are filled with national pride, and therefore we *particularly* hate *our* slavish past . . . and our slavish present, in which the same landowners, aided by the capitalists, lead us into war to stifle Poland and the Ukraine, to throttle the democratic movement in Persia and in China, to strengthen the gang of ·Romanovs, Bobrinskys, Purishkeviches that covers with shame our Great-Russian national dignity."*

This is what Lenin wrote on national pride.

I think, comrades, that when the fascists, at the Leipzig trial, attempted to slander the Bulgarians as a barbarian people, I was not wrong in taking up the defence of the national honour of the toiling masses of the Bulgarian people, who are struggling heroically against the fascist usurpers, the real barbarians and savages, nor was I wrong in declaring that I had no cause to be ashamed of being a Bulgarian but that, on the contrary, I was proud of being a son of the heroic Bulgarian working class.

Comrades, proletarian internationali·m must, so to speak, " acclimatise itself " in each country in order to sink deep roots in its native land. *National forms* of the proletarian class struggle and of the labour movement in the individual countries are in no contradiction to proletarian internationalism; on the contrary, it is precisely in these forms that the *international interests* of the proletariat can be successfully defended.

It goes without saying that it is necessary *everywhere and on all occasions* to expose before the masses and prove to them concretely that on the pretext of defending general

* Lenin, *Collected Works,* Vol. XVIII, pp. 100-01.

national interests, the fascist bourgeoisie is conducting its
egotistical policy of oppressing and exploiting its own people,
as well as robbing and enslaving other nations.   But we must
not *confine ourselves* to this.   We must at the same time
prove by the very struggle of the working class and the
actions of the Communist Parties that the proletariat in
rising against every manner of bondage and national oppression is the *only* true fighter for national freedom and the
independence of the people.

The interests of the class struggle of the proletariat against
its native exploiters and oppressers are in no contradiction
whatever to the interests of a free and happy future of the
nation.   On the contrary, the Socialist revolution will signify
the *saving of the nation* and will open up to it the road to
loftier heights.   By *the very fact* of building at the present
time its class organisations and consolidating its positions, by
the very fact of defending the democratic rights and liberties
against fascism, by the very fact of fighting for the overthrow
of capitalism, the working class is fighting for the future of
the nation.

The revolutionary proletariat is fighting to save the culture
of the people, to liberate it from the shackles of decaying
monopoly capitalism, from barbarous fascism which is
violating it.   *Only* the proletarian revolution can avert the
destruction of culture, and raise it to the highest stage of
flowering as a truly national culture—*national in form and
socialist in content*—which, under *Stalin's* leadership, is
being realised in the Union of Soviet Socialist Republics
before our very eyes.

Proletarian internationalism not only does not contradict
this struggle of the toilers of the individual countries for
national, social and cultural freedom, but, thanks to international proletarian solidarity and fighting unity, provides
the *support* which is necessary for victory in this struggle.
The working class in the capitalist countries can triumph *only
in closest alliance* with the victorious proletariat of the great
Soviet Union.   *Only* by struggling hand in hand with the
proletariat of the imperialist countries can the colonial peoples
and oppressed national minorities achieve their freedom.   The
road to victory for the proletarian revolution in the imperialist
countries lies *only* through the revolutionary alliance of the
working class of the imperialist countries with the national
liberation movement in the colonies and dependent countries,

because, as *Marx* taught us, " no nation can itself be free if it oppresses other nations."

Communists belonging to an oppressed, dependent nation cannot combat chauvinism successfully among the people of their own nation if they *do not at the same time show* in practice, in the mass movement, that they actually struggle for the liberation of their nation from the alien yoke. And again, on the other hand, the Communists of an oppressing nation cannot do what is necessary to educate the toiling masses of their nation in the spirit of internationalism *without waging* a resolute struggle against the oppressor policy of their " own " bourgeoisie and for the right to complete self-determination of the nations kept in bondage by it. If they do not do this, they likewise do not make it easier for the toilers of the oppressed nation to overcome their nationalist prejudices.

If we act in this spirit, if in all our mass work we prove convincingly that we are free of both national nihilism and bourgeois nationalism, then and only then shall we be able to wage a really successful struggle against the chauvinist demagogy of the fascists.

This is the reason why a correct and practical application of the Leninist-Stalinist national policy is of such paramount importance. It is *unquestionably an essential* preliminary condition for a successful struggle against chauvinism—this main instrument of ideological influence of the fascists upon the masses.

III. CONSOLIDATION OF THE COMMUNIST PARTIES AND STRUGGLE FOR THE POLITICAL UNITY OF THE PROLETARIAT.

Comrades, in the struggle for the establishment of the united front the importance of the leading role of the Communist Party increases extraordinarily. Only the Communist Party is at bottom the initiator, the organiser and the driving force of the united front of the working class.

The Communist Parties can ensure the mobilisation of the broadest masses of the toilers for a united struggle against fascism and the offensive of capital *only if they strengthen their own ranks in every respect,* if they develop their initiative, pursue a Marxist-Leninist policy and apply correct, flexible tactics which take into account the concrete situation and alignment of class forces.

Consolidation of the Communist Parties.

In the period between the Sixth and Seventh Congresses, our Parties in the capitalist countries have undoubtedly *grown in stature and have been considerably steeled.* But it would be a most dangerous mistake to rest on this achievement. The more the united front of the working class extends, the more will new, complex problems rise before us and the more will it be necessary for us to work on the political and organisational consolidation of our Parties. The united front of the proletariat brings to the fore an army of workers which will be able to carry out its mission if this army is headed by a leading force which will point out its aims and paths. This leading force can *only be a strong proletarian, revolutionary party.*

If we Communists exert every effort to establish a united front, we do this not for the narrow purpose of recruiting new members for the Communist Parties. But we must strengthen the Communist Parties in every way and increase their membership *for the very reason* that we seriously want to strengthen the united front. The strengthening of the Communist Parties is not a narrow Party concern, but the concern of the entire working class.

The unity, revolutionary coherence and fighting preparedness of the Communist Parties constitute most valuable capital which belongs not only to us but to the entire working class.

We have combined and shall continue to combine our readiness to march jointly with the Social-Democratic Parties and organisations to the struggle against fascism with an irreconcilable struggle against Social-Democracy as the ideology and practice of compromise with the bourgeoisie, and consequently also against *any penetration* of this ideology into our own ranks.

In boldly and resolutely carrying out the policy of the united front, we meet in our own ranks with obstacles which we must remove at all costs in the shortest possible time.

After the Sixth Congress of the Comintern, a *successful struggle was waged* in all Communist Parties of the capitalist countries *against any tendency towards an opportunist adaptation to the conditions of capitalist stabilisation and against any infection with reformist and legalist illusions.* Our Parties purged their ranks of various kinds of Right opportunists, thus strengthening their Bolshevik unity and fighting capacity. Less successful and frequently entirely lacking was the fight against *sectarianism.* Sectarianism manifested itself no longer in primitive, open forms, as in the first years of the existence of the Communist International, but, under cover of a formal recognition of the Bolshevik theses, hindered the development of a Bolshevik mass policy. In our day this is often no longer an " *infantile disorder,*" as Lenin wrote, but a *deeply rooted vice,* which must be shaken off or it will be impossible to solve the problem of establishing the united front of the proletariat and of leading the masses from the positions of reformism to the side of the revolution.

In the present situation sectarianism, *self-satisfied* sectarianism, as we designate it in the draft resolution, *more than anything else* impedes our struggle for the realisation of the united front. Sectarianism, satisfied with its *doctrinaire narrowness,* its divorcement from the real life of the masses; satisfied with its *simplified methods* of solving the most complex problems of the working class movement on the basis of stereotyped schemes; sectarianism which professes to know all and considers it needless to learn from the masses, from the lessons of the labour movement. In short, sectarianism, to which, as they say, mountains are mere stepping-stones.

Self-satisfied sectarianism *will not and cannot* understand that the leadership of the working class by the Communist Party cannot be attained by a process of spontaneous development. The leading role of the Communist Party in the struggles of the working class must be won. For this purpose it is necessary, not to rant about the leading role of the Communists, but to *merit and win the confidence of the working masses* by everyday mass work and correct policy. This will only be possible if we Communists in our political work seriously take into account the actual level of the class consciousness of the masses, the degree to which they have become revolutionised, if we soberly appraise the concrete situation, not on the basis of our wishes but on the basis of the actual state of affairs. Patiently, step by step, we must make it easier for the broad masses to come over to the positions of Communism. We ought never to forget these warning words of Lenin, so forcefully expressed :

" This is the whole point—we must *not* regard that which is obsolete *for us as* being obsolete *for the class,* as being obsolete *for the masses.*"*

Is it not a fact, comrades, that there are still not a few such doctrinaire elements left in our ranks who at all times and places sense nothing but danger in the policy of the united front? For such comrades the whole united front is one unrelieved peril. But this sectarian " stickling for principle " is nothing but political helplessness in face of the difficulties of directly leading the struggle of the masses.

Sectarianism finds expression *particularly* in overestimating the revolutionisation of the masses, in overestimating the speed at which they are abandoning the positions of reformism, in attempts to leap over difficult stages and over complicated tasks of the movement. Methods of leading the masses have in practice been frequently replaced by the methods of leading a narrow party group. The power of traditional contacts between the masses and their organisations and leaders has been underestimated, and when the masses did not break off these contacts immediately, the attitude taken towards them was just as harsh as that adopted towards their reactionary leaders. Tactics and slogans have tended to become stereotyped for all countries, and the specific features of the specific conditions in each individual country have been left out of account. The necessity of stubborn struggle in the very midst of the masses themselves to win their confidence has tended to be ignored, the struggle for the partial demands of the workers and work in the reformist trade

---

* Lenin, *" Left-Wing " Communism, an Infantile Disorder,* p. 55.

unions and fascists mass organisations has been neglected. The policy of the united front has frequently been replaced by bare appeals and abstract propaganda.

In no less a degree have sectarian views hindered the correct selection of people, the training and developing of *cadres connected with the masses, enjoying the confidence* of the masses, cadres whose *revolutionary mettle* has been *tried* and *tested* in class battles, cadres that are capable of combining the practical *experience* of *mass* work with the *staunchness of principle of a Bolshevik.*

Thus sectarianism has to a considerable extent retarded the growth of the Communist Parties, has impeded the prosecution of a real mass policy, prevented our taking advantage of the difficulties of the class enemy to strengthen the positions of the revolutionary movement, hindered the winning over of the broad proletarian masses to the side of the Communist Parties.

While fighting most resolutely to overcome and exterminate the last remnants of self-satisfied sectarianism, we must increase to a maximum our vigilance in regard to and the struggle against *Right opportunism* and against every one of its concrete manifestations, bearing in mind that the danger of Right opportunism will increase in proportion as the wide united front develops more and more. Already there are tendencies to reduce the role of the Communist Party in the ranks of the united front and to effect a reconciliation with Social-Democratic ideology. Nor must the fact be lost sight of that the tactics of the united front are a method of convincing the Social-Democratic workers by object lesson of the correctness of the Communist policy and the incorrectness of the reformist policy, and *that they are not a reconciliation with Social-Democratic ideology and practice.* A successful struggle for the establishment of the united front imperatively demands constant struggle in our ranks against tendencies to *deprecate the role of the Party,* against *legalist illusions,* against reliance on *spontaneity and automatism,* both in the liquidation of fascism and in conducting the united front against the *slightest vacillation at the moment of determined action.*

" It is necessary," Stalin teaches us, " that the Party be able to combine in its work the greatest adhesion to principle (not to be confused with sectarianism !) with a maximum of contacts and connections with the masses (not to be confused with ' tailism !'), without which it is not only impossible for the Party to teach the

masses but also to learn from them, not only to lead the masses
and raise them to the level of the Party, but to listen to the voice
of the masses and divine their sorest needs." (Stalin " The
Perspective of the Communist Party of Germany and Bolshevisa-
tion," *Pravda,* No. 27, February 3, 1925.)

Political Unity of the Working Class.

Comrades, the development of the united front of joint
struggle of the Communist and Social-Democratic workers
against fascism and the offensive of capital likewise brings
to the fore the question of *political unity, of a single political
mass party of the working class.* The Social-Democratic
workers are becoming more and more convinced by experience that the struggle against the class enemy demands
unity of political leadership, inasmuch as *duality in leadership* impedes the further development and reinforcement of
the joint struggle of the working class.

The interests of the class struggle of the proletariat and
the success of the proletarian revolution make it impera-
tive that there be a *single party of the proletariat* in each
country. Of course, it is not so easy or simple to achieve
this. This requires stubborn work and struggle, and will of
necessity be a more or less protracted process. The Communist Parties must, in reliance upon the growing urge
of the workers for a unification of the Social-Democratic
Parties or of individual organisations with Communist
Parties, firmly and confidently take the initiative in this
unification. The cause of amalgamating the forces of the
working class in a single revolutionary proletarian party,
at the time when the international labour movement is entering the period of closing the split in its ranks, is *our cause,*
is the cause of the Communist International.

But while it is sufficient for the establishment of the
united front of the Communist and Social-Democratic Parties
to have an agreement to struggle against fascism, the offensive of capital and war, the achievement of political unity
is possible only on the basis of a number of definite conditions involving principles.

This unification is possible only :

First, on condition of their *complete independence of
the bourgeoisie and the complete rupture of the bloc of
Social-Democracy with the bourgeoisie;*

Second, on condition that unity of action be first brought
about ;

Third, on condition that the necessity of the *revolutionary overthrow of the rule of the bourgeoisie* and the establishment of the *dictatorship of the proletariat in the form of Soviets* be recognised;

Fourth, on condition that support of one's own bourgeoisie *in imperialist war* be rejected;

Fifth, on condition that the Party be constructed on the basis of *democratic centralism,* which ensures unity of will and action, and has been tested by *the experience of the Russian Bolsheviks.*

We must explain to the Social-Democratic workers, patiently and in comradely fashion, why political unity of the working class in impossible without these conditions. We must discuss together with them the sense and significance of these conditions.

Why is it necessary for the realisation of the political unity of the proletariat that there be complete independence of the bourgeoisie and a rupture of the *bloc* of Social-Democrats with the bourgeoisie?

Because the entire experience of the labour movement, particularly the experience of the fifteen years of coalition policy in Germany, has shown that the policy of class collaboration, the policy of dependence on the bourgeoisie, leads to the defeat of the working class and to the victory of fascism. And only the road of irreconcilable class struggle against the bourgeoisie, the road of the Bolsheviks, is the true road to victory.

Why must unity of action be first established as a preliminary condition of political unity?

Because unity of action to repel the offensive of capital and of fascism is possible and necessary even before the majority of the workers are united on a common political platform for the overthrow of capitalism, while the working out of unity of views on the main lines and aims of the struggle of the proletariat, without which a unification of the parties is impossible, requires a more or less extended period of time. And unity of views is worked out best of all in joint struggle against the class enemy *even to-day.* To propose to unite at once instead of forming a united front means to place the cart before the horse and to imagine that the cart will then move ahead. (*Laughter.*) Precisely for the reason that for us the question of political unity is not a manœuvre, as it is for many Social-Democratic leaders, we insist on the realisation of unity of action as one of the most important stages in the struggle for political unity.

Why is it necessary to recognise the revolutionary overthrow of the bourgeoisie and the establishment of the dictatorship of the proletariat in the form of Soviet power?

Because the experience of the victory of the great October Revolution on the one hand, and, on the other, the bitter lessons learned in Germany, Austria and Spain during the entire post-war period have confirmed once more that the victory of the proletariat is possible only by means of the revolutionary overthrow of the bourgeoisie, and that the bourgeoisie would rather drown the labour movement in a sea of blood than allow the proletariat to establish Socialism by peaceful means. The experience of the October Revolution has demonstrated patently that the basic content of the proletarian revolution is the question of the proletarian dictatorship, which is called to crush the resistance of the overthrown exploiters, to arm the revolution for struggle against imperialism and to lead the revolution to the complete victory of Socialism. In order to achieve the dictatorship of the proletariat as the dictatorship of the vast majority over an insignificant minority, over the exploiters—and only as such can it be brought about—for this are needed *Soviets* embracing all strata of the working class, the basic masses of the peasantry and the rest of the toilers, without the awakening of whom, without the inclusion of whom in the front of the revolutionary struggle, the victory of the proletariat cannot be consolidated.

Why is the refusal of support to the bourgeoisie in an imperialist war a condition of political unity?

Because the bourgeoisie wages imperialist war for its predatory purposes, against the interests of the vast majority of the peoples, under whatever guise this war may be waged. Because all imperialists combine their feverish preparations for war with extremely intensified exploitation and oppression of the toilers in their own country. Support of the bourgeoisie in such a war means treason to the country and the international working class.

Why, finally, is the building of the Party on the basis of democratic centralism a condition of unity?

Because only a party built on the basis of democratic centralism can ensure unity of will and action, can lead the proletariat to victory over the bourgeoisie, which has at its disposal so powerful a weapon as the centralised State apparatus. The application of the principle of democratic centralism has stood the splendid historical test of the experience of the Russian Bolshevik Party, the Party of Lenin and Stalin.

Yes, comrades, we are for a single mass political party of the working class. But this party must be, in the words of Comrade Stalin,

" a militant party, a revolutionary party, bold enough to lead the proletarians to the struggle for power, with sufficient experience to be able to orientate itself in the complicated problems that arise in a revolutionary situation, and sufficiently flexible to steer clear of any submerged rocks on the way to its goal."*

This explains why it is necessary to strive for political unity on the basis of the conditions indicated.

We are for the political unity of the working class! Therefore we are ready to collaborate most closely with all Social-Democrats who are for the united front and sincerely support unification on the principles indicated. But precisely because we are for unity, we shall struggle resolutely against all " Left " demagogues who will try to make use of the disillusionment of the Social-Democratic workers to create new Socialist Parties or Internationals directed against the Communist movement, and thus keep deepening the split in the working class.

We welcome the aspiration which is gaining ground among Social-Democratic workers for a united front with the Communists. In this fact we see a growth of their revolutionary consciousness and a beginning of the healing of the split in the working class. Being of the opinion that unity of action is a pressing necessity and the truest road to the establishment of the political unity of the proletariat as well, we declare that the Communist International and its Sections are ready to enter into negotiations with the Second International and its Sections for the establishment of the unity of the working class in the struggle against the offensive of capital, against fascism and the threat of imperialist war.

---

* Stalin, " Foundations of Leninism," *Leninism*, Vol. I, p. 88.

CONCLUSION.

Comrades, I am concluding my report. As you see, we are raising a number of questions to-day in a new light, taking account of the change in the situation since the Sixth Congress and of the lessons of our struggle, and relying on the degree of consolidation in our ranks already achieved, primarily the question of the united front and of the approach to Social-Democracy, the reformist trade unions and other mass organisations.

There are wiseacres who will sense in all this a digression from our basic positions, some sort of turn to the Right of the straight line of Bolshevism. Well, in my country, Bulgaria, they say that a hungry chicken always dreams of millet. Let those political chickens think so.

This interests us little. For us it is important that our own Parties and the broad masses of the whole world should correctly understand what we are striving for.

We would not be revolutionary Marxists, Leninists, worthy pupils of Marx, Engels, Lenin and Stalin, if we did not reconstruct our policies and tactics in accordance with the changing situation and the changes occurring in the labour movement.

We would not be real revolutionaries if we did not learn from our own experience and the experience of the masses.

We want our Parties in the capitalist countries to come out and act as *real political parties of the working class,* to become in actual fact *a political factor* in the life of their countries, to pursue at all times *an active Bolshevik mass policy and not confine themselves to propaganda and criticism, and bare appeals to struggle for proletarian dictatorship.*

We are enemies of all cut-and-dried schemes. We want to take into account the concrete situation at each moment, in each place, and not act *according to a fixed, stereotyped form* anywhere and everywhere; not to forget that in *varying* circumstances the position of the Communists cannot be *identical.*

We want soberly to take into account *all stages* in the development of the class struggle and in the growth of the class consciousness of the masses themselves, to be able to locate and solve at each stage the *concrete* problems of the revolutionary movement *corresponding* to this stage.

We want to find a *common language* with the broadest masses for the purpose of struggling against the class enemy, to find ways of finally overcoming *the isolation of the revolutionary vanguard* from the masses of the proletariat and all other toilers, as well as of overcoming the fatal *isolation of the working class itself* from its natural allies in the struggle against the bourgeoisie, against fascism.

We want to draw increasingly wide masses into the revolutionary class struggle and lead them to proletarian revolution, *proceeding from their vital interests and needs as the starting point, and their own experience as the basis.*

Following the example of our glorious Russian Bolsheviks, the example of the leading Party of the Communist International, the Communist Party of the Soviet Union, we want to combine the *revolutionary heroism* of the German, the Spanish, the Austrian and other Communists *with genuine revolutionary realism,* and put an end to the last remnants of scholastic tinkering with serious political questions.

We want to equip our Parties from every angle for the solution of the most complex political problems confronting them. For this purpose we want to raise ever higher their *theoretical level,* to train them in the spirit of live Marxism-Leninism and not dead doctrinairism.

We want to eradicate from our ranks all *self-satisfied sectarianism,* which above all blocks our road to the masses and impedes the carrying out of a truly Bolshevik mass policy. We want to intensify in every way the struggle against all concrete manifestations of *Right opportunism,* realising that the danger from this side will increase precisely in the practice of carrying out our mass policy and struggle.

We want the Communists of each country promptly to draw and apply *all the lessons* that can be drawn from their own experience as the revolutionary vanguard of the proletariat. We want them *as quickly as possible to learn how to sail on the turbulent waters of the class struggle,* and not to remain on the shore as observers and registrars of the surging waves in the expectation of fine weather.

This is what we want!

And we want all this because only in this way will the working class at the head of all the toilers, welded into a million-strong revolutionary army, led by the Communist International and possessed of so great and wise a pilot as our leader Comrade Stalin, be able to fulfil its historical mission with certainty—to sweep fascism off the face of the earth and, together with it, capitalism!

Speech in Reply to Discussion

Comrades ! The very full discussion on my report shows the immense interest taken by the Congress in the fundamental tactical problems and tasks of the struggle of the working class against the offensive of capital and fascism, against the threat of imperialist war.

Summing up the eight-day discussion we can state that all the principal propositions contained in the report have met with the unanimous approval of the Congress. None of the speakers objected to the tactical line we have proposed or to the resolution which has been submitted.

I venture to say that at none of the previous Congresses of the Communist International has such ideological and political solidarity been revealed as at the present Congress. The complete unanimity displayed at the Congress indicates that the necessity of revising our policy and tactics in accordance with the changed conditions and with due regard for the most abundant and instructive experience of the past few years, has come to be fully recognised in our ranks.

This unanimity may undoubtedly be regarded as one of the most important prerequisites for success in solving the paramount immediate problem of the international proletarian movement, namely, *establishing unity of action of all sections of the working class in the struggle against fascism.*

The successful solution of this problem requires, first, that Communists skilfully wield the weapon of *Marxist-Leninist analysis,* while carefully studying the specific conditions and the alignment of class forces as they develop, and plan their activity and struggle accordingly. We must mercilessly root out the weakness, not infrequently observed in our comrades, for cut-and-dried schemes, lifeless formulas and ready-made patterns. We must put an end to the state of affairs in which Communists, when lacking the knowledge or ability for Marxist-Leninist analysis, substitute general phrases and slogans such as " the revolutionary way out of the crisis," without making the slightest serious attempt to explain the conditions, the relationship of class forces, the degree of revolutionary maturity of the proletariat and the

toiling masses, and the level of influence of the Communist
Party necessary to render such a revolutionary way out of
the crisis possible.   Without such an analysis all these catch-
words become "dud" shells, empty phrases which only
obscure our tasks of the day.   Without a concrete Marxist-
Leninist analysis we shall never be able correctly to present
and solve the problem of fascism, the problem of the proletarian front and the general people's front, the problem of
our attitude towards bourgeois-democracy, the problem of
the processes going on within the working class, particularly
among the Social-Democratic workers, the problem of a
united front government, or any of the numerous other new
and complex problems with which life itself and the development of the class struggle confronts us now and will confront us in the future.

Second, we need *live people*—people who have grown
up from the masses of the workers, have sprung from their
everyday struggle, people of militant action wholeheartedly
devoted to the cause of the proletariat, people whose brains
and hands will give effect to the decisions of our Congress.
Without Bolshevik, Leninist-Stalinist cadres we shall be
unable to solve the enormous problems that confront the
toilers in the fight against fascism.

Third, we need people equipped with the *compass of
Marxist-Leninist theory*, for people who are unable to make
skilful use of this instrument slip into narrow, make-shift
politics, take decisions only from case to case, and lose the
broad perspective of the struggle which shows the masses
where we are going and whither we are leading the toilers.

Fourth, we need the *organisation of the masses* in order to
put our decisions into practice.   Our ideological and political
influence alone is not enough.   We must put a stop to reliance on *spontaneity in the movement* (on the hope that the
movement would develop of its own accord), which is one
of our fundamental weaknesses.   We must remember that
without persistent, prolonged, patient, and sometimes
apparently thankless organisational work on our part, the
masses will never make for the Communist shore.   In order
to be able to organise the masses we must acquire Lenin's
and Stalin's art of making our decisions the property not
only of the Communists but also of the broadest masses of
the toilers.   We must learn to talk to the masses, not in the
language of book formulas, but in the language of fighters in

the cause of the masses, whose every word, whose every idea reflects the innermost thoughts and sentiments of millions.

It is with these problems that I should like to deal in my closing speech.

Comrades! The Congress has welcomed the new tactical lines with great enthusiasm and unanimity. Enthusiasm and unanimity are all very well, of course; but it is still better when these are combined with a well-considered and critical approach to the tasks that confront us, with a proper comprehension of the decisions adopted and a real understanding of the means and methods by which these decisions are to be applied to the particular circumstances of each country.

After all, we have before now unanimously adopted good resolutions, but the trouble was that not infrequently after adopting these decisions, we at best made them the property of only the small vanguard of the working class. These decisions did not become flesh and blood of the broad masses; they did not become a guide to the action of the millions.

Can we assert that we have already finally abandoned this formal approach to adopted decisions? No. It must be said that even at this Congress the speeches of some of the comrades gave indication of remnants of formalism; a desire made itself felt at times to substitute for the concrete analysis of reality and life's experience some sort of new scheme, some sort of new, over-simplified lifeless formula, to represent as *actually existing* what we *desire*, but does *not yet exist*.

The Struggle Against Fascism Must be Made Concrete.

No general characterisation of fascism, however correct in itself, can relieve us of the need to study and take into account the specific development of fascism and the various forms of fascist dictatorship in the individual countries and at its various stages. It is necessary in each country to investigate, study and ascertain the national peculiarities, the specific national features of fascism and map out accordingly effective methods and forms of struggle against fascism.

Lenin persistently warned us against " stereotyped methods and mechanical levelling, against rendering tactical rules, rules of struggle, identical." This warning is particularly to the point when it is a question of fighting an enemy who so subtly and Jesuitically exploits the national sentiments and prejudices of the masses and their anti-capitalist inclinations in the interests of big capital. *Such an enemy must be known to perfection, from every angle.* We must without any delay whatever react to his various manœuvres, discover his hidden moves, be prepared to repel him in any arena and at any moment. We must not hesi-tate even to *learn* from the enemy if that will help us more quickly and more effectively *to wring his neck.*

It would be a gross mistake to lay down a universal rule of development of fascism, to cover all countries and all peoples. Such a rule would not help, but hamper us in carrying on a real struggle. Apart from everything else, such a rule would result in indiscriminately thrusting into the camp of fascism those sections of the population which, if properly approached, could, at a certain stage of develop-ment, be brought into the struggle against fascism, or could at least be neutralised.

Let us take, for example, the development of fascism in France and in Germany. Some comrades believe that, generally speaking, fascism cannot develop as easily in France as in Germany. What is true and what is false in this contention ? It is true that there were no such deep-seated democratic traditions in Germany as there are in France, which went through several revolutions in the eighteenth and nineteenth centuries. It is true that France is a country which won the war and forced the Versailles system on other countries, that the national sentiments of the French people have not been hurt as they have been in Ger-many where this factor played such a great part. It is true that in France the basic masses of the peasantry are pro-Republic and anti-fascist, especially in the South, in con-trast with Germany where even before fascism came to power a considerable section of the peasantry was under the influence of reactionary parties.

But, comrades, notwithstanding the existing differences in the development of the fascist movement in France and in Germany, notwithstanding the factors which impede the onslaught of fascism in France, it would be shortsightedness not to notice the uninterrupted growth there of the fascist peril and to under-estimate the possibility of a fascist *coup d'état.* Moreover, a number of factors in France favour the development of fascism. One must not forget that the

economic crisis, which commenced later in France than in
other capitalist countries, continues to deepen and sharpen,
and this greatly facilitates the orgy of fascist demagogy.
French fascism holds strong positions in the army, among
the officers, such as the Nationalist Socialists did not have
in the Reichswehr before their advent to power. Furthermore, in no other country, perhaps, has the parliamentary
regime been corrupted to such an enormous extent and
caused such indignation among the masses as in France.
Nor must it be forgotten that the development of fascism is
furthered by the French bourgeoisie's keen fear of losing its
political and military hegemony in Europe.

Hence it follows that the successes scored by the anti-
fascist movement in France, of which Comrades Thorez and
Cachin have spoken here, and over which we so heartily
rejoice, are still far from indicating that the toiling masses
have definitely succeeded in blocking the road to fascism. I
must emphatically stress once more the full importance of the
tasks of the French working class in the struggle against
fascism, of which I already spoke in my report.

It would likewise be dangerous to cherish illusions
regarding the weakness of fascism in other countries where
it does not enjoy a broad mass base. We have the example
of such countries as Bulgaria, Yugoslavia and Finland,
where fascism, although it had no broad base, came to
power, relying on the armed forces of the state, and then
sought to broaden its base by making use of the State
apparatus.

Comrade Dutt was right in his contention that there was
a tendency amongst us to contemplate fascism in general,
without taking into account the specific features of the fascist
movement in the various countries, erroneously classifying
all reactionary measures of the bourgeoisie as fascism and
going as far as calling the entire non-Communist camp
fascist. The struggle against fascism was not strengthened
but rather weakened in consequence.

Even now we still have survivals of a stereotyped
approach to the question of fascism. When some comrades
assert that Roosevelt's " New Deal " represents an ever
clearer and more pronounced form of the development of the
bourgeoisie towards fascism than the " National Government " in Great Britain, for example, is this not a manifestation of such a stereotyped approach to the question? One

must indeed be a confirmed addict of the use of hackneyed
schemes not to see that the most reactionary circles of
American finance capital which are attacking Roosevelt represent first and foremost the very force which is stimulating
and organising the fascist movement in the United States.
Not to see the beginnings of real fascism in the United States
behind the hypocritical outpourings of these circles " in
defence of the democratic rights of the American citizen " is
tantamount to misleading the working class in the struggle
against its worst enemy.

In the colonial and semi-colonial countries there can be
no question of the kind of fascism that we are accustomed
to see in Germany, Italy and other capitalist countries. Here
we must study and take into account the quite different
economic, political and historical conditions, in accordance
with which fascism is assuming, and will continue to assume,
peculiar forms of its own.

Unable to approach the phenomena of real life concretely.
some comrades, who suffer from mental laziness, substitute
general, non-committal *formulas* for a careful and concrete
study of the *actual* situation and the relationship of class
forces.   Unlike *snipers* who shoot with unerring aim, they
remind us of those " crack " riflemen who regularly and
unfailingly *miss* the target, shooting either too high or too
low, too near or too far.   But we, comrades, as Communists,
active in the labour movement, as the revolutionary vanguard of the working class, want to be snipers who unfailingly *hit* the target.

The United Proletarian Front and the Anti-Fascist People's Front.

Some comrades are quite needlessly racking their brains
over the problem of *what to begin with—the united proletarian front or the anti-fascist people's front*.

Some say that we cannot start forming the anti-fascist
people's front until we have organised a solid united front
of the proletariat.

Others argue that, since the establishment of the united
proletarian front meets with the resistance of Social-Democracy in a number of countries, it is better to start at once
with building up the people's front, and then develop the
united working-class front on this basis.

Evidently both groups fail to understand that the united
proletarian front and the anti-fascist people's front are inter-

connected and interwoven, the one passing into the other in the process of the practical struggle against fascism as a consequence of the *living dialectics of the struggle,* and that there is certainly no Chinese wall to keep them apart.

For it cannot be seriously supposed that it is impossible to establish a genuine anti-fascist people's front without securing the unity of action of the working class itself, the *guiding force* of this anti-fascist people's front. At the same time, the further development of the united proletarian front depends, to a considerable degree, upon its transformation into a people's front against fascism.

Comrades! Just picture to yourselves a devotee of cut-and-dried theories of this kind, gazing upon our resolution and contriving his pet scheme with the zeal of a true pedant:

First, local united proletarian front from below;

Then, regional united front from below;

Thereafter, united front from above, passing through the same stages;

Then, unity in the trade union movement;

After that, the enlistment of other anti-fascist parties;

This to be followed by the extended people's front, from above and from below;

After which the movement must be raised to a higher level, politicalised, revolutionised, and so on and so forth. (Laughter.)

You will say, comrades, that this is sheer nonsense. I agree with you. But the unfortunate thing is that in some form or other this kind of sectarian nonsense is still to be found quite frequently in our ranks.

How does the matter really stand? Of course, we must strive everywhere for a broad anti-fascist people's front of struggle against fascism. But in a number of countries we shall not get beyond general talk about the people's front, unless we succeed in mobilising the masses of the workers for the purpose of breaking down the resistance of Social-Democracy to the formation of a proletarian united front of struggle. This is how the matter stands, above all in Great Britain where the working class comprises the majority of the population and where the bulk of the working class follows the lead of the trade unions and the Labour Party. That is how matters stand in Belgium and in the Scandinavian countries where the numerically small Communist

Parties must face strong mass trade unions and numerically
large Social-Democratic Parties.

In these countries the Communists would commit a very
serious political mistake if they shirked the struggle to establish a united proletarian front under cover of general talk
about a people's front which cannot be formed without the
participation of the mass working-class organisations. In
order to bring about a genuine people's front in these countries, the Communists must carry out an enormous amount
of political and organisational work among the masses of
the workers. They must overcome the preconceived ideas
of these masses who regard their mass reformist organisations as already the embodiment of proletarian unity. They
must convince these masses that the establishment of a
united front with the Communists means a shift on the part
of those masses to the position of the class struggle, and that
this shift alone will guarantee success in the struggle against
the offensive of capital and fascism. We shall not overcome
these difficulties by setting ourselves much wider tasks here.
On the contrary, in fighting to remove these difficulties we
shall thus actually, and not in words alone, prepare the
ground for the creation of a genuine people's front of battle
against fascism, against the capitalist offensive and against
the threat of imperialist war.

The issue is a different one in countries like Poland, where
a strong peasant movement is developing side by side with
the labour movement, where the peasant masses have their
own organisations which are becoming radicalised as a result
of the agrarian crisis, where national oppression evokes
indignation among the national minorities. Here the
development of the general people's front of struggle will
proceed parallel with the development of the united proletarian front, and at times in this type of country the movement for a general people's front may even outstrip the
movement for a working-class front.

Take a country like Spain, which is in the process of a
bourgeois-democratic revolution. Can it be said that,
because the proletariat is split up into numerous small organisations, complete fighting unity of the working class
must first be established here before a workers' and peasants'
front against Lerroux and Gil Robles is created? By
tackling the question in this way we would isolate the proletariat from the peasantry, would in effect be withdrawing the

slogan of the agrarian revolution, would make it easier for the enemies of the people to disunite the proletariat and the peasantry, and set the peasantry in opposition to the working class. Yet this, comrades, as is well known, was one of the main reasons why the working class was defeated in the October events of 1934.

However, one thing must not be forgotten : in all countries where the proletariat is comparatively small in numbers, where the peasantry and the urban petty-bourgeois strata predominate, it is all the more necessary to bend every effort to set up a firm united front of the working class itself, so that it may be able to take its place as the leading factor with regard to all the toilers.

Thus, comrades, in attacking the problem of the proletarian front and the people's front, there can be no general panacea suitable for all cases, all countries, all peoples. In this matter universalism, the application of one and the same recipe to all countries is equivalent, if you will allow me to say so, to ignorance, and ignorance should be flogged, even when it stalks about, nay, particularly when it stalks about, in the cloak of universal cut-and-dried schemes.

The Rôle of Social-Democracy and its Attitude Towards the United Front of the Proletariat.

Comrades, in view of the tactical problems confronting us, it is very important to give a correct reply to the question of whether Social-Democracy at the present time is still the principal bulwark of the bourgeoisie, and if so, where?

Some of the comrades who participated in the discussion (Comrades Florin, Dutt) touched upon this question, but in view of its importance a fuller reply must be given to it, for it is a question which workers of all trends, particularly Social-Democratic workers, are asking and cannot help asking.

It must be borne in mind that in a number of countries the position of Social-Democracy in the bourgeois state, and its attitude towards the bourgeoisie, have been undergoing a change.

In the first place, the crisis has thoroughly shaken the position of even the most secure section of the working class, the so-called aristocracy of labour, upon which, as we know, Social-Democracy relies for support. This section, too, is beginning more and more to revise its views as to the expediency of the policy of class collaboration with the bourgeoisie.

Second, as I pointed out in my report, the bourgeoisie in a number of countries is itself compelled to abandon bourgeois democracy and resort to the terroristic form of its dictatorship, depriving Social-Democracy not only of its previous position in the political system of finance capital, but also, under certain conditions, of its legal status, persecuting and even suppressing it.

Third, under the influence of the lessons learnt from the defeat of the workers in Germany, Austria and Spain, a defeat which was largely the result of the Social-Democratic policy of class collaboration with the bourgeoisie, and, on the other hand, under the influence of the victory of Socialism in the Soviet Union as a result of Bolshevik policy and the application of living, revolutionary Marxism, the Social-Democratic workers are becoming revolutionised, are beginning to turn to the class struggle against the bourgeoisie.

The joint effect of all this has been to make it increasingly difficult and in some countries actually impossible, for Social-Democracy to preserve its former role of bulwark of the bourgeoisie.

Failure to understand this is particularly harmful in those countries in which the fascist dictatorship has deprived Social-Democracy of its legal status. From this point of view the self-criticism of those German comrades, who in their speeches mentioned the necessity of ceasing to cling to the letter of obsolete formulas and decisions concerning Social-Democracy, of ceasing to ignore the changes that have taken place in its position, was correct. It is clear that if we ignore these changes, it will lead to a distortion of our policy in favour of establishing the unity of the working class, and will facilitate the sabotage of the united front by the reactionary elements of the Social-Democratic leaders.

The process of revolutionisation in the ranks of the Social-Democratic Parties now going on in all countries is developing unevenly. It must not be imagined that the Social-Democratic workers who are becoming revolutionised will *at once* and on a mass scale adopt the position of consistent class struggle, and will *straightway* unite with the Communists without any intermediate stages. In a number of countries this will be a more or less difficult, a

more or less complicated and prolonged process, essentially
dependent, at any rate, on the correctness of our policy and
tactics. We must even reckon with the possibility that, in
passing from the position of class collaboration with the
bourgeoisie to the position of class struggle against the
bourgeoisie, some Social-Democratic Parties and organisations will continue to exist for a time as independent organisations or parties. In such event there can, of course, be
no thought of such Social-Democratic organisations or
parties being regarded as a bulwark of the bourgeoisie.

It cannot be expected that those Social-Democratic
workers who are under the influence of the ideology of class
collaboration with the bourgeoisie, which has been instilled
in them in the course of decades, will part with this ideology
of their own accord, actuated solely by objective causes. No.
It is our business, the business of the Communists, to help
them free themselves from the hold of reformist ideology.
The work of explaining the principles and programme of
Communism must be carried on patiently, in a comradely
fashion, and must be adapted to the degree of development
of the individual Social-Democratic workers. Our criticism
of Social-Democracy must become more specific and
systematic, and must be based on the experience of the
Social-Democratic masses themselves.

It must be borne in mind that primarily by utilising their
experience in the joint struggle with the Communists
against the class enemy will it be possible and necessary to
facilitate and accelerate the revolutionary development of the
Social-Democratic workers. There is no more effective
means of the Social-Democratic workers abandoning their
vacillation and doubts than participation in the proletarian
united front.

We shall do all in our power to make it easier, not only
for the Social-Democratic workers, but also for those leading
members of Social-Democratic Parties and organisations
who sincerely desire to adopt the revolutionary class position,
to work and fight with us against the class enemy. At the
same time we declare that any Social-Democratic func-
tionary, lower official, or worker who continues to uphold the
disruptive tactics of the reactionary Social-Democratic
leaders, who come out against the united front and thus
directly or indirectly aid the class enemy, will thereby incur
at least equal guilt before the working class as those who are

historically responsible for having supported the Social-
Democratic policy of class collaboration, the policy which in
a number of European countries doomed the revolution in
1918 and cleared the way for fascism.

The attitude adopted towards the united front is the divi-
ding line between the reactionary sections of Social-Democracy and the sections that are becoming revolutionary. Our
assistance to the latter will be the more effective, the more
we intensify our fight against the reactionary camp of
Social-Democracy participating in a bloc with the
bourgeoisie. And within the Left camp the self-determination of the various elements will take place the sooner, the
more determinedly the Communists fight for a united front
with the Social-Democratic Parties. The experience of the
class struggle and the participation of the Social Democrats
in the united front movement will show who in that camp
will prove to be " left " merely in words and who is really
Left.

The United Front Government.

While the attitude of Social-Democracy towards the practical realisation of the united proletarian front is, generally
speaking, the principal indication in every country of
whether the previous role in the bourgeois state of the Social-
Democratic Party or of its individual parts has changed, and
if so, to what extent, the *attitude of the Social-Democrats on
the issue of a united front government will be a particularly
clear test.*

When a situation arises in which the question of creating
a united front government becomes an immediate practical
problem, this issue will become decisive, the touchstone for
the policy of Social-Democracy in the given country : either
jointly with the fascist-bound bourgeoisie against the working class, or jointly with the revolutionary proletariat against
fascism and reaction, not alone in words but in deeds. That
is how the question will inevitably be presented at the time
the united front government is formed as well as while it
is in power.

I think that enough was said in my report about the
character of the united front government and the anti-fascist
people's front government, as well as the conditions of their
formation, to provide general tactical direction. To expect
us over and above this to indicate all possible forms and all

conditions under which such governments may be formed would mean but to invite futile conjecture.

I would like to utter a note of warning against over-simplification or the application of any hard-and-fast rules in this question. Life is more complex than any scheme. For example, it would be wrong to imagine that the united front government is an *indispensable stage* on the road to the establishment of the proletarian dictatorship. That is just as wrong as the former assertion that there will be *no intermediary stages* in the fascist countries and that fascist dictatorship is *certain to be immediately* superseded by proletarian dictatorship.

The whole question boils down to this : will the proletariat itself be prepared at the decisive moment for the direct overthrow of the bourgeoisie and the establishment of its own power, and will it be able in that event to secure the support of its allies ? Or, will the movement of the united proletarian front and the anti-fascist people's front at the particular stage be in a position only to suppress or overthrow fascism, without directly proceeding to abolish the dictatorship of the bourgeoisie ? In the latter case it would be an intolerable piece of political shortsightedness, and not serious revolutionary politics, to use this alone as a ground for refusing to create and support a united front or a people's front government.

It is likewise not difficult to understand that the establishment of a united front government in countries where fascism is not yet in power is something *different* from the creation of such a government in countries where the fascist dictatorship holds sway.   In the latter countries a united front government can be created *only in the process of overthrowing fascist rule.* In countries where the *bourgeois-democratic revolution* is developing, a people's front government may become the government of the democratic dictatorship of the working class and the peasantry.

As I have already pointed out in my report, the Communists will do all in their power to support a united front government to the extent that the latter will really fight against the enemies of the people and grant freedom of action to the Communist Party and to the working class. The question of whether Communists will take part in the government will be determined entirely by the actual situation pre-

vailing at the time. Such questions will be settled as they
arise. No handy recipes can be prescribed in advance.

Attitude Towards Bourgeois Democracy.

Comrade Lenski pointed out in his speech that " while
mobilising the masses to repel the onslaught of fascism
against the rights of the toilers, the Polish Party at the same
time had its misgivings about formulating positive democratic demands in order not to create democratic illusions
among the masses." The Polish Party is, of course, not
the only one in which such fear of formulating positive
democratic demands exists in one way or another.

Where does that fear come from, comrades? It comes
from an incorrect, non-dialectical conception of our attitude
towards bourgeois democracy. We, Communists, are
unswerving upholders of Soviet democracy, the great proto-
type of which is the proletarian dictatorship in the Soviet
Union where the introduction of equal suffrage, and the
direct and secret ballot is proclaimed by resolution of the
Seventh Congress of Soviets at the same time that the last
vestiges of bourgeois democracy are being wiped out in the
capitalist countries. This Soviet democracy presupposes the
victory of the proletarian revolution, the conversion of pri-
vate property in the means of production into public
property, the embarking of the overwhelming majority of
the people on the road to Socialism. This democracy does
not represent a final form; it develops and will continue
to develop in proportion as further progress is made in
Socialist construction, in the creation of classless society and
in the overcoming of the survivals of capitalism in economic
life and in the minds of the people.

But to-day the millions of toilers living under capitalism
are faced with the necessity of taking a definite stand on
these forms in which the *rule of the bourgeoisie* is clad in the
various countries. We are not anarchists and it is not at all
a matter of indifference to us what kind of political regime
exists in any given country: whether a bourgeois dictatorship in the form of bourgeois democracy, even with
democratic rights and liberties greatly curtailed, or a bourgeois dictatorship in its open, fascist form. Being upholders
of Soviet democracy, *we shall defend every inch of the
democratic gains which the working class has wrested in the
course of years of stubborn struggle, and shall resolutely
fight to extend these gains.*

How great were the sacrifices of the British working class before it secured the right to strike, a legal status for its trade unions, the right of assembly and freedom of the press, extension of the franchise, and other rights! How many tens of thousands of workers gave their lives in the revolutionary battles fought in France in the nineteenth century to obtain the elementary rights and the lawful opportunity of organising their forces for the struggle against the exploiters. The proletariat of all countries has shed much of its blood to win bourgeois-democratic liberties, and will naturally fight with all its strength to retain them.

Our attitude towards bourgeois democracy is not the same under all conditions. For instance, at the time of the October Revolution, the Russian Bolsheviks engaged in a life-and-death struggle against all political parties which opposed the establishment of the proletarian dictatorship under the slogan of the defence of bourgeois democracy. The Bolsheviks fought these parties because the banner of bourgeois democracy had at that time become the standard around which all counter-revolutionary forces mobilised to challenge the victory of the proletariat. The situation is quite different in the capitalist countries at present. Now the fascist counter-revolution is attacking bourgeois democracy in an effort to establish a most barbaric regime of exploitation and suppression of the toiling masses. Now the toiling masses in a number of capitalist countries are faced with the necessity of making a *definite* choice, and of making it to-day, not between proletarian dictatorship and bourgeois democracy, but between bourgeois democracy and fascism.

Besides, we have now a situation which differs from that which existed, for example, in the epoch of capitalist stabilisation. At that time the fascist danger was not as acute as it is to-day. At that time it was bourgeois dictatorship in the form of bourgeois democracy that the revolutionary workers were facing in a number of countries and it was against bourgeois democracy that they were concentrating their fire. In Germany, they fought against the Weimar Republic, not because it was a republic, but because it was a *bourgeois* republic, which was suppressing the revolutionary movement of the proletariat, especially in 1918-20 and in 1923.

But could the Communists maintain this stand also when the fascist movement began to raise its head, when, for

instance, in 1932, the fascists in Germany were organising
and arming hundreds of thousands of storm troopers against
the working class? Of course not. It was the mistake of
the Communists in a number of countries, particularly in
Germany, that they failed to take into account the changes
which had taken place, but continued to repeat those slogans,
maintain those tactical positions which had been correct a
few years before, especially when the struggle for the proletarian dictatorship was an immediate issue, and when the
entire German counter-revolution was rallying under the
banner of the Weimar Republic, as it did in 1918-20.

And the circumstances that even to-day we must still make
reference to fear, in our ranks, of launching positive democratic slogans indicates how little our comrades have mastered
the Marxist-Leninist method of approaching such important
problems of our tactics. Some say that the struggle for
democratic rights may divert the workers from the struggle
for the proletarian dictatorship. It may not be amiss to
recall what Lenin said on this question:

" It would be a fundamental mistake to suppose that the
struggle for democracy can divert the proletariat from the Socialist
revolution, or obscure, or overshadow it, etc. On the contrary,
just as socialism cannot be victorious unless it introduces complete democracy, so the proletariat will be unable to prepare for
victory over the bourgeoisie unless it wages a many-sided, consistent and revolutionary struggle for democracy."*

These words should be firmly fixed in the memories of
all our comrades, bearing in mind that in history the great
revolutions have grown out of small movements for the
defence of the elementary rights of the working class. But
in order to be able to link up the struggle for democratic
rights with the struggle of the working class for Socialism,
it is necessary first and foremost to discard any cut-and-
dried approach to the question of defence of bourgeois
democracy.

A Correct Line Alone Is Not Enough.

Comrades, it is clear, of course, that for the Communist
International and each of its Sections, the fundamental thing
is to work out a correct line. But a correct line alone is
not enough for concrete leadership in the class struggle.

* Lenin, *Selected Works,* Vol. V., p. 268.

For that, a number of conditions must be fulfilled, above all the following:

First, *organisational guarantees* that adopted decisions will be carried out in practice and that all obstacles in the way will be resolutely overcome. What Comrade Stalin said at the Seventeenth Congress of the Communist Party of the Soviet Union about the conditions necessary to carry out the line of the Party, can and should bear, in its entirety, also on the decisions which our Congress adopts.

Comrade Stalin said:

" Some people think that it is sufficient to draw up a correct Party line, proclaim it from the housetops, enunciate it in the form of general theses and resolutions and carry them unanimously in order to make victory come of itself, automatically, so to speak. This, of course, is wrong. Those who think like that are greatly mistaken. Only incorrigible bureaucrats and office rats can think that. As a matter of fact, these successes and victories were obtained, not automatically, but as a result of a fierce struggle to carry out the Party line. Victory never comes by itself—it has to be dragged by the hand. Good resolutions and declarations in favour of the general line of the Party are only a beginning; they merely express the desire to win, but it is not victory. After the correct line has been given, after a correct solution of the problem has been found, success depends on the manner in which the work is organised, on the organisation of the struggle for the application of the line of the Party, on the proper selection of workers, on supervising the fulfilment of the decisions of the leading organs. Without this the correct line of the Party and the correct solutions are in danger of being severely damaged. More than that, after the correct political line has been given, the organisational work decides everything, including the fate of the political line itself, *i.e.*, whether it is fulfilled or not."*

It is hardly necessary to add anything to these striking words of Comrade Stalin, which must become a guiding principle in all the work of our Parties.

Another condition is the *ability to convert decisions of the Communist International and its Sections into decisions of the broad masses themselves.* This is all the more necessary now when we are faced with the task of organising a united front of the proletariat and drawing the broad masses of the people into an anti-fascist people's front. The political and

---

* Stalin, " Report on the Work of the Central Committee." See *Socialism Victorious,* pp. 78-9.

tactical genius of *Lenin* and *Stalin* is evinced most clearly and most vividly in their masterful ability to get the masses to understand the correct line and the slogans of the Party through their own experience. If we follow up the history of Bolshevism, that greatest of treasure houses of the political strategy and tactics of the revolutionary movement, we can see for ourselves that the Bolsheviks never substituted methods of leading the Party for methods of leading the masses.

Comrade Stalin pointed out that one of the peculiarities of the tactics of the Russian Bolsheviks in the period of preparation for the October Revolution consisted in their ability correctly to determine the path and the turns which naturally lead the masses to the slogans of the Party, to the very " threshold of the revolution," helping them to sense, to test and to realise from their own experience the correctness of these slogans. They did not confuse leadership of the Party with leadership of the masses, but clearly saw the difference between leadership of the first kind and leadership of the second kind. In this way they worked out tactics as the science, not only of Party leadership, but also of the leadership of the millions of toilers.

Furthermore, it must be borne in mind that *the broad masses cannot assimilate our decisions unless we learn to speak the language which the masses understand.* We do not always know how to speak simply, concretely, in images which are familiar and intelligible to the masses. We are still loath to dispense with abstract formulas which we have learnt by rote. As a matter of fact, if you scan our leaflets, newspapers, resolutions and theses, you will find that they are often written in a language and style so heavy that they are difficult for even our Party functionaries to understand, let alone the rank-and-file workers.

If we reflect, comrades, that workers, especially in fascist countries, who distribute or only read these leaflets risk their very lives by doing so, we shall realise still more clearly the need of writing for the masses in a language which they understand, so that the sacrifices made may not have been in vain.

The same applies in no less degree to our oral agitation and propaganda. We must admit quite frankly that in this respect the fascists have often proven more dexterous and flexible than many of our comrades.

I recall, for example, a meeting of unemployed in Berlin before Hitler's accession to power. It was at the time of the trial of those notorious swindlers and speculators, the Sklarek brothers, which dragged on for several months. A National Socialist speaker in addressing the meeting made demagogic use of that trial, to further his own ends. He referred to the swindles, the bribery and other crimes committed by the Sklarek brothers, emphasised that the trial had been dragging for months and figured out how many hundreds of thousands of marks it had already cost the German people. To the accompaniment of loud applause the speaker declared that such bandits as the Sklarek brothers should have been shot without any ado, and the money wasted on the trial should have gone to the unemployed.

A Communist rose and asked for the floor. The chairman at first refused to recognise him, but under the pressure of the audience which wanted to hear from the Communists he had to let him speak. When the Communist got upon the platform everybody awaited with tense expectation what the Communist speaker would have to say. Well, what did he say?

" Comrades," he began in a loud and strong voice, " the Plenum of the Communist International has just closed. It showed the way to the salvation of the working class. The chief task it puts before you, comrades, is ' *to win the majority of the working class.* . . .' The Plenum pointed out that the unemployed movement must be ' politicalised.' The Plenum calls on us to raise it *to a higher level.*"

He went on in the same strain, evidently under the impression that he was " explaining " authentic decisions of the Plenum.

Could such a speech appeal to the unemployed? Could they find any satisfaction in the fact that first we intended to politicalise, then revolutionise, and finally mobilise them in order to raise their movement to a higher level?

Sitting in a corner of the hall, I observed with chagrin how the unemployed, who had been so eager to hear a Communist in order to find out from him what to do concretely, began to yawn and display unmistakable signs of disappointment. And I was not at all surprised when towards the end the chairman rudely cut our speaker short without any protest from the meeting.

This unfortunately is not the only case of its kind in our

agitational work. Nor were such cases confined to Germany. To agitate in such fashion means to agitate against one's own cause. It is high time to put an end once and for all to these, to say the least, childish methods of agitation.

During my report, the chairman, Comrade Kuusinen, received a characteristic letter from the floor of the Congress addressed to me. Let me read it:

" In your speech at the Congress, please take up the following question, namely, that all resolutions and decisions adopted in the future by the Communist International be written so that not only trained Communists can get the meaning, but that any working man reading the material of the Comintern might without any preliminary training be able to see at once what the Communists want, and of what service Communism is to mankind. Some Party leaders forget this. They must be reminded of it, and very strongly, too. Also that agitation for Communism be conducted in understandable language."

I do not know exactly who is the author of this letter, but I have no doubt that this comrade voiced in his letter the opinion and desire of millions of workers. Many of our comrades think that the more high-sounding words, and the more formulas and theses unintelligible to the masses they use, the better their agitation and propaganda, forgetting that the greatest leaders and theoreticians of the working class of our epoch, *Lenin* and *Stalin,* have always spoken and written in highly popular language, readily understood by the broad masses.

Everyone of us must make this a law, a Bolshevik law, an elementary rule:

When writing or speaking always have in mind the rank-and-file worker, who must understand you, must believe in your appeal and be ready to follow you! You must have in mind those for whom you write, to whom you speak.

Cadres*

Comrades, our best resolutions will remain scraps of paper if we lack the people who are to put them into effect. Unfortunately, however, I must state that the problem of *cadres,* one of the most important questions that confront us, received practically no attention at this Congress. The report of the Executive Committee of the Communist Inter-

---

* Cadres—here referring to active Party workers and functionaries, or officials.—*Transl.*

national was discussed for seven days. There were many
speakers from various countries, but only a few, and they
only in passing, discussed this question, so extremely vital
for the Communist Parties and the labour movement. In
their practical work our Parties have not yet realised by far
that *people, cadres, decide everything*. They are unable to
do what Comrade *Stalin* taught us to do, namely, cultivate
cadres " as a gardener cultivates his favourite fruit tree,"
" to appreciate people, to appreciate cadres, to appreciate
every worker who can be of use to our common cause."

An indifferent attitude on the question of cadres is all
the more impermissible for the reason that we are constantly
losing some of the most valuable of our cadres in the
struggle.   For we are not a learned society but a militant
movement which is constantly on the firing line.   Our most
energetic,   most   courageous   and   most   class-conscious
elements are in the front ranks.   It is precisely these front-
line men that the enemy hunts down, murders, throws into
jail, puts in concentration camps and subjects to excruciating
torture, particularly in fascist countries.   This creates the
very urgent necessity of constantly replenishing the ranks,
cultivating and training new cadres as well as carefully preserving the existing cadres.

The question of cadres is of particular urgency for the
additional reason that under our influence the mass united
front movement is gaining momentum and bringing forward
many thousands of new working-class militants.   Moreover,
it is not only young revolutionary elements, not only workers
just becoming revolutionary, who have never before participated in a political movement, that stream into our ranks.
Very often former members and activists of the Social-Democratic Parties also join us.   These new cadres require special
attention, particularly in the illegal Communist Parties, the
more so because these cadres with their poor theoretical
training   frequently   come   up   against   serious   political
problems in their practical work which they must solve for
themselves.

The   problem   of   what shall be the *correct policy with
regard to cadres* is a very serious one for our Parties, as well
as for the Young Communist Leagues and for all other mass
organisations—for the entire revolutionary labour movement.

What does a correct policy with regard to cadres imply?

First, *knowing one's people*. As a rule there is no systematic study of cadres in our Parties. Only recently have the Communist Parties of France and Poland and, in the East, the Communist Party of China, achieved certain successes in this direction. The Communist Party of Germany, before its underground period, had also undertaken a study of its cadres. The experience of these Parties has shown that as soon as they began to study their people, Party workers were discovered who had remained unnoticed before. On the other hand, the Parties began to be purged of alien elements who were ideologically and politically harmful. It is sufficient to point to the example of Celor and Barbé in France who, when put under the Bolshevik microscope turned out to be agents of the class enemy and were thrown out of the Party. In Poland and in Hungary the verification of cadres made it easier to discover nests of provocateurs, agents of the enemy, who had sedulously concealed their identity.

Second, *proper promotion of cadres*. Promotion should not be something casual but one of the normal functions of the Party. It is bad when promotion is made exclusively on the basis of narrow Party considerations, without regard to whether the Communist promoted has contact with the masses or not. Promotion should take place on the basis of the ability of the various Party workers to discharge particular functions, and of their popularity among the masses. We have examples in our Parties of promotions which have produced excellent results. For instance, we have a Spanish woman-Communist, sitting in the Presidium of this Congress, Comrade Dolores. Two years ago she was still a rank-and-file Party worker. But in the very first clashes with the class enemy she proved to be an excellent agitator and fighter. Subsequently promoted to the leading body of the Party, she has proved herself a most worthy member of that body.

I could point to a number of similar cases in several other countries, but in the majority of cases promotions are made in an unorganised and haphazard manner, and therefore are not always fortunate. Sometimes moralisers, phrasemongers and chatterboxes who actually harm the cause are promoted to leading positions.

Third, *the ability to use people to best advantage*. We must be able to ascertain and utilise the valuable qualities of every single active worker. There are no ideal people; we must take them as they are and correct their weaknesses and shortcomings. We know of glaring examples in our Parties of the wrong utilisation of good, honest Communists who might have been very useful had they been given work that they were better fit to do.

Fourth, *proper distribution of cadres.* First of all, we must see to it that the main links of the movement are in the charge of strong people who have contacts with the masses, have sprung from the very depths of the masses, who have initiative and are staunch. The more important districts should have an appropriate number of such activists. In capitalist countries it is not an easy matter to transfer cadres from one place to another. Such a task encounters a number of obstacles and difficulties, including lack of funds, family considerations, etc., difficulties which must be taken into account and properly overcome. But usually we neglect to do this altogether.

Fifth, *systematic assistance to cadres.* This assistance should take the form of careful instruction, comradely control, rectification of shortcomings and mistakes and concrete, everyday guidance.

Sixth, *proper care for the preservation of cadres.* We must learn promptly to withdraw Party workers to the rear whenever circumstances so require, and replace them by others. We must demand that the Party leadership, particularly in countries where the Parties are illegal, assume paramount responsibility for the preservation of cadres. The proper preservation of cadres also presupposes highly efficient organisation of secrecy in the Party. In certain of our Parties many comrades think that the Parties are sufficiently prepared for underground existence even though they have reorganised themselves only formally, according to ready-made rules. We had to pay very dearly for having started the real work of reorganisation only after the Party had gone underground, under the direct heavy blows of the enemy. Remember the severe losses the Communist Party of Germany suffered during its transition to underground conditions! Its experience should serve as a serious warning to those of our Parties which to-day are still legal but may lose their legal status to-morrow.

Only a correct policy in regard to cadres will enable our Parties to develop and utilise all available forces to the utmost, and obtain from the enormous reservoir of the mass movement ever fresh reinforcements of new and better active workers.

What should be our *main criteria* in selecting cadres?

First, *absolute* devotion to the cause of the working class, *loyalty to the Party,* tested in face of the enemy—in battle, in prison, in court.

Second, the closest possible *contact with the masses*. The comrades concerned must be wholly absorbed in the interests of the masses, feel the life pulse of the masses, know their sentiments and requirements. The prestige of the leaders of our Party organisation should be based, first of all, on the fact that the masses regard them as their leaders, and are convinced through their own experience of their ability as leaders, and of their determination and self-sacrifice in struggle.

Third, *ability independently to find one's bearings* and not to be afraid of *assuming responsibility in taking decisions*. He who fears to take responsibility is not a leader. He who is unable to display literature, who says : " I will do only what I am told," is not a Bolshevik. Only he is a real Bolshevik leader who does not lose his head at moments of defeat, who does not get a swelled head at moments of success, who displays indomitable firmness in carrying out decisions. Cadres develop and grow best when they are placed in the position of having to solve concrete problems of the struggle independently, and are aware that they are fully responsible for their decisions.

Fourth, *discipline* and *Bolshevik hardening* in the struggle against the class enemy as well as in their irreconcilable opposition to all deviations from the Bolshevik line.

We must place all the more emphasis on these conditions which determine the correct selection of cadres, because in practice preference is very often given to a comrade who, for example, may be able to write well and be a good speaker but is not a man or woman of action, is not as suited for the struggle as some other comrade who perhaps may not be able to write or speak so well, but is a staunch comrade, possessing initiative and contacts with the masses, and is capable of going into battle and leading others into battle. Have there not been ever so many cases of sectarians, doctrinaires or moralisers crowding out loyal mass workers, genuine working-class leaders?

Our leading cadres should combine the knowledge of *what* they must do—with *Bolshevik stamina, revolutionary strength of character and the will power to carry it through.*

In connection with the question of cadres permit me, comrades, to dwell also on the great role which the *International Labour Defence* is called upon to play in relation to the cadres of the labour movement. The material and moral assistance which the I.L.D. organisations render to our prisoners and their families, to political emigrants, to persecuted revolutionaries and anti-fascists, has saved the lives and preserved the strength and fighting capacity of thousands upon thousands of most valuable fighters of the working class in many countries. Those of us who have been in jail have found out directly through our own experience the enormous significance of the activity of the I.L.D.

By its activity, the I.L.D. has won the affection, attachment and profound gratitude of hundreds of thousands of proletarians, and of revolutionary elements among the peasantry and professional people. It must become, so to speak, a sort of " Red Cross " of the united front of the proletariat and the anti-fascist people's front, embracing millions of toiling people—the " Red Cross " of the army of the toiling classes embattled against fascism fighting for peace and socialism. If the I.L.D. is to perform its part successfully, it must train thousands of its own active militants, a multitude of *I.L.D. workers* of its own, answering in their character and capacity the *special purposes* of this extremely important organisation.

Under present conditions when bourgeois reaction is growing, when fascism is raging and the class struggle is becoming more acute, the role of the I.L.D. is increasing immensely. The task now before the I.L.D. is to become a genuine mass organisation of the toilers in all capitalist countries (particularly in fascist countries where it must adapt itself to the special conditions prevailing there).

And here I must say as categorically and as sharply as I possibly can that while a *bureaucratic* approach and a soulless attitude toward people is despicable in the labour movement taken in general, in the sphere of activity of the

I.L.D. such an attitude is an evil bordering on the criminal. The fighters of the working class, the victims of reaction and fascism who are suffering agony in torture chambers and concentration camps, political emigrants and their families should all meet with the most sympathetic care and solicitude on the part of the organisation and functionaries of the I.L.D. The I.L.D. must still better appreciate and discharge its duty of assisting the fighters in the proletarian and anti-fascist movement, particularly in physically and morally preserving the cadres of the labour movement. The Communists and revolutionary workers who are active in the I.L.D. organisations must realise at every step the enormous responsibility they bear before the working class and the Communist International for the successful fulfilment of the role and tasks of the I.L.D.

Comrades, as you know, cadres receive their best training *in the process of struggle,* in surmounting difficulties and withstanding tests, in studying *favourable* and *unfavourable* examples of conduct. We have hundreds of examples of splendid conduct in times of strikes, during demonstrations, in jail, in court. We have thousands of instances of heroism, but unfortunately also not a few cases of pigeon-heartedness, lack of firmness, and even desertion. We often forget these examples, both good and bad. We do not teach people to benefit by these examples. We do not show them what should be emulated and what rejected. We must study the conduct of our comrades and active workers during class conflicts, at police court hearings, in the jails and concentration camps, in court, etc. The good sides should be brought to light and held up as models to be followed, while all that which is rotten, non-Bolshevik and philistine is to be cast aside. Since the Leipzig trial we have had quite a number of comrades appearing before bourgeois and fascist courts who have shown that numerous cadres are growing up with an excellent understanding of *what* really constitutes Bolshevik conduct in court.

But how many even of you delegates to the Congress know the details of the trial of the railwaymen in Rumania, know about the trial of Fiete Schulz who was subsequently beheaded by the fascists in Germany, the trial of our valiant Japanese comrade, Itikawa, the trial of the Bulgarian revolutionary soldiers, and many other trials at which admirable examples of proletarian heroism were displayed? Such worthy examples of proletarian heroism must be popularised, must be contrasted with the manifestations of faintheartedness, philistinism, and every kind of rot and frailty in our ranks and the ranks of the working class. These examples must be used most extensively in educating the cadres of the labour movement.

Comrades! Our Party leaders often complain that *there are no people;* that they are short of people for agitational and propaganda work, for the newspapers, the trade unions, for work among the youth, among women. Not enough, not enough—that is the cry. We simply haven't got the people. To this we could reply in the old, yet eternally new, words of Lenin:

" *There are no people—yet there are enormous numbers of people.* There are enormous numbers of people, because the working class and the most diverse strata of society, year after year, advance from their ranks an increasing number of discontented people who desire to protest, who are ready to render all the assistance they can in the fight against absolutism, the intolerableness of which is not yet recognised by all, but is nevertheless more and more acutely sensed by increasing masses of the people. At the same time we have no people, because we have no leaders, no political leaders, we have no talented organisers capable of organising extensive and at the same time uniform and harmonious work that would give employment to all forces, even the most inconsiderable."[*]

These words of Lenin must be thoroughly grasped by our Parties and applied by them as a guide in their everyday work. There are plenty of people. They need only be discovered in our own organisations, during strikes and demonstrations, in various mass organisations of the workers, in united front bodies. They must be helped to grow in the course of their work and struggle; they must be put in such conditions where they can really be useful to the workers' cause.

Comrades, we Communists are people of action. Ours is the problem of practical struggle against the offensive of capital, against fascism and the threat of imperialist war, the struggle for the overthrow of capitalism. It is precisely

---

[*] Lenin, " What Is to be Done?" *Selected Works,* Vol. II., p. 142.

this *practical* task that imposes upon the Communist cadres the obligation to equip themselves with *revolutionary theory*. For us *Stalin*, that greatest master of revolutionary action, has taught us; theory gives those engaged in practical work the power of orientation, clarity of vision, assurance in work, belief in the triumph of our cause.

But real revolutionary theory is irreconcilably hostile to any emasculated theorising, any futile toying with abstract definitions. *Our theory is not a dogma, but a guide to action,* Lenin used to say. It is *such* a theory that our cadres need, and they need it as badly as they need their daily bread, as they need air, water. Whoever really wishes to rid our work of deadening, stereotyped schemes, of pernicious scholasticism, must sear them out with a red-hot iron, both by real, *practical,* active struggle waged together with and at the head of the masses, and by untiring effort to grasp the mighty, fertile, all-powerful Bolshevik theory, the teaching of Marx, Engels, Lenin, Stalin.

In this connection I consider it particularly necessary to draw your attention to the work of our *Party schools*. It is not pedants, moralisers or adepts at quoting that our schools must train. No! It is practical front-rank fighters in the cause of the working class that must leave their walls —people who are front-rank fighters not only because of their boldness and readiness for self-sacrifice, but also because they see further than rank-and-file workers and know better than they the path that leads to the emancipation of the toilers. All sections of the Communist International must without any dilly-dallying seriously take up the question of the proper organisation of Party schools, in order to turn them into *smithies,* where these fighting cadres are to be forged.

The principal task of our Party schools, it seems to me, is to teach the Party and Young Communist League members there how to apply the Marxist-Leninist method to the concrete situation in particular countries, to definite conditions, not to the struggle against an enemy " in general " but against a particular, definite enemy. For this purpose it is necessary to study not merely the letter of Leninism, but its living revolutionary spirit.

There are two ways of training cadres in our Party schools :

First method: teaching people abstract theory, trying to give them the greatest possible dose of dry learning, coaching them how to write theses and resolutions in literary style, and only incidentally touching upon the problems of the particular country of the particular labour movement, its history and traditions, and the experience of the Communist Party in question. Only incidentally!

Second method: such theoretical training in the fundamental principles of Marxism-Leninism as is based on a practical study by the student of the cardinal problems concerning the struggle of the proletariat in his own country. On returning to his practical work, the student will then be able to find his bearings independently, and *become an independent practical organiser and leader capable of leading the masses to battle against the class enemy.*

Not all graduates of our Party schools prove to be suitable timber. Many have phrases, abstractions, book knowledge and show of learning. But we need real, truly Bolshevik organisers and leaders of the masses. And we need them badly this very day. It does not matter if such students be unable to write good theses (though we need that very much, too) as long as they know how to organise and lead, undaunted by difficulties, capable of surmounting them.

Revolutionary theory is the generalised, *summarised experience* of the revolutionary movement. Communists must carefully utilise in their countries not only the experience of the past but, also the experience of the present struggle of other detachments of the international labour movement. However, correct utilisation of experience does not by any means denote *mechanical transposition* of ready-made forms and methods of struggle from one set of conditions to another set, from one country to another, as so often happens in our Parties. Bare imitation, simple copying of methods and forms of work, even of the Communist Party of the Soviet Union in countries where capitalism is still supreme, may with the best of intentions result in harm rather than good, as has so often actually been the case. It is precisely from the experience of the Russian Bolsheviks that we must learn to apply effectually, to the specific conditions of life in each country, the *single international line;* in the struggle against capitalism we must learn pitilessly to cast aside, pillory and hold up to general ridicule all *phrase-mongering, use of hackneyed formulas, pedantry and doctrinairism.*

It is necessary to learn, comrades, to learn always, at every step, in the course of the struggle, at liberty and in jail. To learn and to fight, to fight and to learn. We must be able to combine the great teaching of Marx, Engels, Lenin, and Stalin *with Stalin's firmness* at work and in struggle, *with Stalin's irreconcilability, on matters of principle,* toward the class enemy and deviators from the Bolshevik line, *with Stalin's fearlessness in face of difficulties, with Stalin's revolutionary realism.*

Comrades! Never has any international congress of Communists aroused such keen interest on the part of world public opinion as we witness now in regard to our present Congress. We may say without fear of exaggeration that there is not a single serious newspaper, not a single political party, not a single more or less serious political or public personage that is not following the course of our Congress with the closest attention.

The eyes of millions of workers, peasants, small townspeople, office workers and intellectuals, of colonial peoples and oppressed nationalities are turned towards Moscow, the great capital of the *first* but not *last* state of the international proletariat.

In this we see a confirmation of the enormous importance and urgency of the questions discussed at the Congress and of its decisions. The frenzied howls of the fascists of all countries, particularly of German fascism fuming at the mouth, only confirm us in our belief that our decisions have indeed hit the mark.

In the dark night of bourgeois reaction and fascism, in which the class enemy is endeavouring to keep the toiling masses of the capitalist countries, the Communist International, the international Party of the Bolsheviks, stands out like a beacon, showing all mankind the one right way to emancipation from the yoke of capitalism, from fascist barbarity and the horrors of imperialist war.

The establishment of unity of action of the working class is a *decisive* stage on that road. Yes, unity of action by the organisations of the working class of every trend, the consolidation of its forces in all spheres of its activity and at all sectors of the class struggle.

The working class must achieve the unity of its *trade
unions*.   In vain do some reformist trade union leaders
attempt to frighten the workers with the spectre of a trade
union democracy destroyed by the interference of the Communist Parties in the affairs of the united trade unions, by
the existence of Communist fractions within the trade unions.

To depict us Communists as opponents of trade union
democracy is sheer nonsense. We advocate and consistently
uphold the right of the trade unions to decide their problems for themselves. We are even prepared to forgo the
idea of creating Communist fractions in the trade unions
if that is necessary to promote trade union unity.   We are
prepared to come to terms as to the independence of the
united trade unions of all political parties.   But we are
decidedly opposed to any *dependence* of the trade unions on
the bourgeoisie, and do not give up our basic point of view
that it is impermissible for trade unions to adopt a *neutral*
position in regard to the class struggle between the proletariat and the bourgeoisie.

The working class must strive to secure the *amalgamation*
of all forces of the working-class youth and of all organisations of the anti-fascist youth, and win over that section of
the toiling youth which has come under the demoralising
influence of fascism and other enemies of the people.

The working class must and will achieve unity of action
in all spheres of the labour movement.   This will come
about the sooner the more firmly and resolutely we Communists and revolutionary workers of all capitalist countries
apply in practice the new tactical line adopted by our Congress in relation to the most important urgent questions of
the international labour movement.

We know that there are many difficulties ahead.   Our
path is not a smooth, asphalt road; our path is not strewn
with roses.   The working class will have to overcome many
an obstacle, obstacles in its own midst, as well; it still faces
the task above all of rendering completely harmless the disruptive role of the reactionary elements of Social-Democracy.
Many are the sacrifices that will be exacted under the hammer
blows of bourgeois reaction and fascism.   The revolutionary
ship of the proletariat will have to navigate among a multitude of submerged rocks before reaching safe port.

But the working class in the capitalist countries is to-day

no longer what it was in 1914, at the beginning of the imperialist war, nor what it was in 1918, at the end of the war. The working class has behind it twenty years of rich experience and revolutionary trials, bitter lessons of a number of defeats, especially in Germany, Austria and Spain.

The working class has before it the inspiring example of the Soviet Union, the country of socialism victorious, an example of how the class enemy can be defeated, of how the working class can establish its own government and build socialist society.

The bourgeoisie no longer holds *undivided* dominion over the whole expanse of the world. Now *the victorious working class* rules over one-sixth of the globe, and Soviets control a vast stretch of territory in the great land of China.

The working class possesses a firm, well-knit revolutionary vanguard, the Communist International. It has a tried and recognised, a great and wise leader—*Stalin.*

The entire course of historical development, comrades, favours the cause of the working class. In vain are the efforts of the reactionaries, the fascists of every hue, the entire world bourgeoisie, to turn back the wheel of history. No, that wheel is turning forward and will continue to turn forward until a world-wide Union of Soviet Socialist Republics shall have been established, until the final victory of Socialism throughout the whole world.

There is but one thing that the working class of the capitalist countries still lacks—unity in its own ranks.

So let the clarion call of Marx and Engels, Lenin and Stalin, the batte cry of the Communist International, ring out all the more loudly from this platform to the whole world :

Workers of the World, Unite!

Speech Concluding the Congress

Comrades, the work of the Seventh World Congress of the Communist International, the Congress of the Communists of all countries, of all continents of the world is coming to a close.

What are the results of this Congress, what is its significance for our movement, for the working class of the world, for the toilers of every land?

It has been the Congress of the complete triumph of the unity between the proletariat of the country of victorious socialism, the Soviet Union, *and the proletariat of the capitalist countries which is still fighting for its liberation.* The victory of socialism in the Soviet Union—a victory of world-historic significance—gives rise in all capitalist countries to a powerful movement towards socialism. This victory strengthens the cause of peace among peoples, enhancing as it does the international importance of the Soviet Union and its role as the mighty bulwark of the toilers in their struggle against capital, against reaction and fascism. It strengthens the Soviet Union as the base of the world proletarian revolution. It sets in motion throughout the whole world not only the workers who are turning more and more to communism, but also millions of peasants and farmers, of the hardworking petty townsfolk, a considerable proportion of the intellectuals, the enslaved peoples of the colonies. It inspires them to struggle, increases their attachment for the great fatherland of all the toilers, strengthens their determination to support and defend the proletarian state against all its enemies.

This victory of socialism increases the confidence of the international proletariat in its own forces and in the tangible possibility of its own victory, a confidence which is itself becoming a tremendously effective force against the rule of the bourgeoisie.

The union of forces of the proletariat of the Soviet Union and of the militant proletariat and toiling masses in the capitalist countries holds out the great perspective of the oncoming collapse of capitalism and the guarantee of the victory of socialism throughout the whole world.

Our Congress has laid down the foundations for *so extensive a mobilisation of the forces of all toilers against capitalism as never existed in the history of the working-class struggle.*

Our Congress has set before the international proletariat as its most important immediate task that of consolidating its forces politically and organisationally, of putting an end to the isolation to which it had been reduced by the Social-Democrat'c policy of class-collaboration with the bourgeoisie, of rallying the toilers around the working class in a wide people's front against the offensive of capital and reaction, against fascism and the threat of war in each individual country and in the international arena.

We have not invented this task. It has been prompted by the experience of the world labour movement itself, above all the experience of the proletariat of France. The great service which the French Communist Party performed consists in the fact that it grasped the need of the hour, that it paid no heed to the sectarians who tried to hold back the Party and hamper the realisation of the united front of struggle against fascism, but acted boldly and in a Bolshevik fashion and, by its pact with the Socialist Party providing for joint action, prepared the united front of the proletariat as the basis for the anti-fascist people's front now in the making. By this action, which accords with the vital interests of all the toilers, the French workers, both Communists and Socialists, have once more advanced the French labour movement to first place, to a leading position in capitalist Europe, and have shown that they are worthy successors of the Communards, worthy exponents of the glorious heritage of the Paris Commune.

It is the great service of the French Communist Party and the French proletariat that by their fighting against fascism in a united proletarian front they helped to prepare the decisions of our Congress, which are of such tremendous importance for the workers of all countries.

But what has been done in Franch constitutes only initial steps. Our Congress, in mapping out the tactical line for the years immediately ahead, could not confine itself to merely recording this experience. It went further. We, Communists, are a class party, a proletarian party. But as the vanguard of the proletariat we are ready to arrange joint actions between the proletariat and the other toiling classes, interested in the fight against fascism. We, Communists, are a revolutionary party; but we are ready to undertake joint action with other parties fighting against fascism.

We, Communists, have other ultimate aims than these classes and parties, but in struggling for our aims we are ready to fight jointly for any immediate tasks which when realised will weaken the position of fascism and strengthen the position of the proletariat.

We, Communists, employ methods of struggle which differ from those of the other parties; but while using our own methods in combating fascism, we, Communists, will also support the methods of struggle used by other parties, however inadequate they may seem to be, if these methods are really directed against fascism.

We are ready to do all this because, in countries of bourgeois-democracy, we want to bar the road to reaction and the offensive of capital and fascism, prevent the abrogation of bourgeois-democratic liberties, forestall fascism's terrorist vengeance upon the proletariat, the revolutionary section of the peasantry and the intellectuals, save the young generation from physical and spiritual degeneracy.

We are ready to do all this because in the fascist countries we want to prepare and hasten the overthrow of fascist dictatorship.

We are ready to do all this *because we want to save the world from fascist barbarity and the horrors of imperialist war.*

Ours is a Congress of struggle for the preservation of peace, against the threat of imperialist war.

We are now raising the issue of this struggle *in a new way.* Our Congress is decidedly opposed to the fatalistic outlook on the question of imperialist war emanating from old Social-Democratic notions.

It is true that imperialist wars are the product of capitalism, that only the overthrow of capitalism will put an end to all war; but it is likewise true that the toiling masses can obstruct imperialist war by their militant action.

To-day the world is not what it was in 1914.

To-day on one-sixth part of the globe there exists a powerful proletarian state that relies on the material strength of victorious socialism. Guided by Stalin's wise peace policy, the Soviet Union has already more than once brought to nought the aggressive plans of the instigators of war.

To-day the world proletariat, in its struggle against war, has at its disposal not only its weapon of mass action, as it did in 1914. To-day the mass struggle of the international working class against war is coupled with the political influence of the Soviet Union as a state, of its powerful Red Army, the most important guardian of the peace.

To-day the working class is not labouring under the exclusive influence of Social-Democracy participating in a bloc with the bourgeoisie, as was the case in 1914. To-day there is the World Communist Party, the Communist International. To-day the bulk of the Social-Democratic workers are turning to the Soviet Union, to its policy of peace, to a united front with the Communists.

To-day the peoples of the colonial and semi-colonial countries do not regard their liberation as a hopeless cause. On the contrary, they are passing on more and more to determined struggle against the imperialist enslavers. The best evidence of this is the Soviet revolution in China and the heroic exploits of the Red Army of the Chinese people.

The popular hatred of war is constantly gaining in depth and intensity. In pushing the toilers into the abyss of imperialist wars the bourgeoisie is staking its head. To-day not only the working class, the peasantry and other toilers champion the cause of the preservation of peace, but also the oppressed nations and weak peoples whose independence is threatened by new wars. Even some of the big capitalist states, afraid of losing out in a new redivision of the world, are interested at the present stage in the avoidance of war.

This gives rise to the possibility of forming a most extensive front of the working class, of all the toilers, and of entire nations against the threat of imperialist war. Relying on the peace policy of the Soviet Union and the will of millions upon millions of toilers to have peace, our Congress has opened up the perspective of unfolding a wide anti-war front not only for the Communist vanguard but for the working class of the whole world, for the peoples of every land. The extent to which this world-wide front is realised and put into action will determine whether the fascist and other imperialist war incendiaries will be able in the near future to kindle a new imperialist war, or whether their fiendish hands will be hacked off by the axe of a powerful anti-war front.

Ours is the Congress of the unity of the working class, the Congress of struggle for a united proletarian front.

We entertain no illusions on the subject of the difficulties which the reactionary portion of the Social-Democratic leaders will place in the path of realising a united proletarian front. But we do not fear these difficulties. For we reflect the will of millions of workers; we serve the interests of the proletariat best by fighting for a united front; and the united front is the surest road to the overthrow of fascism and the capitalist order of society, to the prevention of imperialist war.

At the Congress we have raised aloft the banner of *trade union unity*. Communists do not insist on the independent existence of the Red trade unions at all costs. We, Communists, want trade union unity. But this unity must be based on actual class struggle and put an end, once and for all, to a situation in which the most consistent and determined advocates of trade union unity and of the class struggle are expelled from the trade unions of the Amsterdam International.

We know that as yet not all those working in the trade unions affiliated with the Red International of Labour Unions have understood and assimilated this line of the Congress. Among these workers there are still remnants of sectarian self-satisfaction which must be overcome if the line of the Congress is to be carried out firmly. But we shall carry out this line whatever the cost, and shall find a common language with our class brothers, our comrades in the struggle, the workers now affiliated with the Amsterdam International.

At this Congress we have taken the course of forming a single mass political party of the working class, to end the political split in the ranks of the proletariat, a split caused by the class-collaboration policy of the Social-Democratic Parties. To us the political unity of the working class is not a manœuvre but a question of the future fate of the entire labour movement. Should there be any people in our midst who approach the question of the political unity of the working class as a manœuvre, we shall fight them as people bringing harm to the working class. Precisely because our attitude on this question is one of absolute seriousness and sincerity, dictated by the interests of the proletariat, we lay down definite fundamental conditions to serve as the basis for such unity. We have not invented these fundamental conditions. They are the result of the experience gained from the sufferings of the proletariat in the course of its struggle; they are also in accordance with the will of millions of Social-Democratic workers, a will engendered by the lessons of the defeats suffered. These fundamental conditions have been tested by the experience of the entire revolutionary labour movement.

Since proletarian unity has been the keynote of our Congress, it has been not only a Congress of the Communist vanguard, but a Congress of the entire international working class thirsting for militant trade union and political unity.

Though our Congress was not attended by delegates of the Social-Democratic workers nor by non-party delegates, though the workers herded into fascist organisations were not represented, the Congress has spoken not only for the Communists but also for these millions of workers. It has expressed the thoughts and feelings of the overwhelming majority of the working class. If the labour organisations of various trends were to hold a really free discussion of our decisions among the workers of the whole world, there is no doubt in our minds but that they would support the decisions for which you, comrades, have voted with such unanimity.

So much the greater our duty as Communists to render the decisions of our Congress in actual fact the property of the entire working class. To have voted for these decisions is not enough. Nor is it enough to popularise them among the members of the Communist Parties. We want the workers affiliated with the parties of the Second International and the Amsterdam Trade Union Federation as well as the workers affiliated with organisations of other political trends to discuss these decisions jointly with us, bring in their amendments and make practical proposals; we want them to deliberate jointly with us how these decisions can best be carried into life, how they can best realise them in practice jointly with us, hand in hand.

Ours has been a Congress of a new tactical orientation for the Communist International.

Standing firmly on the impregnable position of Marxism-

Leninism, which has been confirmed by the entire experience of the international labour movement, and primarily by the victories of the great October Revolution, our Congress, acting in the spirit and guided by the method of living Marxism-Leninism, has revised the tactical lines of the Communist International to meet the changed world situation.

The Congress has taken a firm decision that the united front tactics must be applied in a new way. The Congress is emphatic in its demands that Communists do not content themselves with the mere propaganda of general slogans about proletarian dictatorship and Soviet power, but that they pursue a definite, active, Bolshevik policy with regard to all internal and foreign political questions arising in their country, with regard to all urgent problems that affect the vital interests of the working class, of their own people and of the international labour movement. The Congress insists most emphatically that all tactical steps taken by the Communist Parties be based on a sober analysis of actual conditions, on a consideration of the relationship of class forces, and of the political level of the broadest masses. The Congress demands the complete eradication of every vestige of sectarianism from the practice of the Communist movement, as this represents at present the greatest obstacle in the way of the Communist Parties carrying out a really mass, really Bolshevik policy.

While imbued with the determination to carry out this tactical line and filled with the conviction that this road will lead our Parties to major successes, the Congress has at the same time taken into account the possibility that the carrying out of this Bolshevik line may not always be smooth sailing, may not always proceed without mistakes, without deviations here and there to the Right or to the " Left "—deviations in the direction of adjusting oneself to trailing behind events, or in the direction of sectarian self-isolation. Which of these is, " speaking generally," the main danger is a dispute in which only scholastics can engage. The greater and worse danger is that which at any given moment and in any given country represents the greater obstacle to the carrying out of the line of our Congress, to the development of the correct mass policy of the Communist Parties.

The cause of Communism demands not abstract but concrete struggle against deviations; the prompt and determined rebuff of all harmful tendencies, as they arise, and the timely rectification of mistakes.   To replace the necessary concrete struggle against deviations by a peculiar sport—hunting imaginary deviations or deviators—is an intolerably harmful twist.   In our Party practice every encouragement must be given to develop initiative in formulating new questions.   We must assist in having the questions concerning the activity of the Party discussed from every angle, and not hastily set down as some deviation or other every doubt or critical remark made by a Party member with reference to practical problems of the movement.   A comrade who committed an error must be given an opportunity to correct it in practice, and only those who stubbornly persist in their mistakes and those who disorganise the Party *are to be flayed without mercy.*

Championing, as we do, working-class unity, we shall with so much the more energy and irreconcilability fight for *unity within our Parties.* There can be no room in our Parties for factions, or for attempts at factionalism.   Whoever will try to break up the iron unity of our ranks by any kind of factionalism will get to feel what is meant by the Bolshevik discipline that Lenin and Stalin have always taught us. Let this be a warning to those few elements in individual parties who think that they can take advantage of the difficulties of their Party, the wounds of defeat or the blows of the raging enemy, to carry out their factional plans, to further their own group interests. *The Party is above everything else! To guard the Bolshevik unity of the Party as the apple of one's eye—is the first and highest law of Bolshevism!*

Ours is a Congress of Bolshevik self-criticism and of the strengthening of the leadership of the Communist International and its Sections.

We are not afraid of pointing out openly the mistakes, weaknesses and shortcomings in our ranks, for we are a revolutionary party which knows that it can develop, grow and accomplish its task only if it discards everything impeding its development as a revolutionary party.

And the work which the Congress has accomplished by its merciless criticism of self-satisfied sectarianism of the use of cut-and-dried schemes and stereotyped practices, phlegmatic thinking, substitution of the methods of leading

a party for the methods of leading masses—all this work
must be continued in an appropriate manner in all Parties,
locally, in all links of our movement, as this is one of the
most essential preconditions for correctly carrying into life
the decisions of the Congress.

In its resolution on the report of the Executive Committee,
the Congress resolved to concentrate *the day-to-day leadership* of our movement in the Sections themselves. This makes
it our duty to intensify in every way the work of forming and
training cadres and of reinforcing the Communist Parties with
genuine Bolshevik leaders, so that at abrupt turns of events
the Parties may quickly and independently find correct
solutions for the political and tactical problems of the Communist movement, on the basis of the decisions of the
Congresses of the Communist International and the Plenums
of its Executive Committee. The Congress, when electing
the leading bodies of the Communist International, strove to
constitute its leadership of such people as accept the new
lines and decisions of the Congress and are ready and able
firmly to carry them into life, not from a sense of discipline,
but out of profound conviction.

It is likewise necessary in each country to ensure the correct application of the decisions adopted by the Congress.
This will depend primarily on appropriately testing, distri-
buting and directing the cadres. We know that this is not
an easy task. It must be borne in mind that some of our
cadres did not go through the experience of the Bolshevik
mass policy, but were brought up largely along the lines of
general propaganda. We must do everything to help our
cadres reorganise, to be retrained in a new spirit, in the spirit
of the decisions of *this Congress.* But where the *old bottles*
prove unsuited for the *new wine,* the necessary conclusions
must be drawn—not to spill the *new wine* or spoil it by pour-
ing it into *old* bottles, but to replace the *old* bottles by *new*
ones.

We intentionally expunged from the reports as well as
from the decisions of the Congress *high-sounding phrases*
on the revolutionary perspective. We did this not because
we have any ground for appraising the tempo of revolutionary
development less optimistically than before, but because we
want to rid our Parties of any inclination to replace Bolshevik
activity by revolutionary phrase-mongering or futile disputes

about the appraisal of the perspective. Waging a decisive struggle against any reliance on spontaneity, we take account of the process of development of the revolution, not as passive observers, but as active participants in this process. By proceeding as the party of revolutionary action—fulfilling at every stage of the movement the tasks that are in the interest of the revolution, the tasks that correspond to the specific conditions of the given stage, and soberly taking into consideration the political level of the wide toiling masses—we accelerate, more than in any other way, the creation of the subjective preconditions necessary for the *victory of the proletarian revolution.*

" *Take things as they are,*" said Marx, " that is, defend the interests of the revolution as changed conditions may require." This is the gist of the matter. This we must never forget.

Comrades! The decisions of the World Congress must be brought home to the masses, must be explained to the masses, must be applied as a guide for the action of the masses, in a word, must be made the flesh and blood of millions of toilers!

It is necessary to encourage everywhere as much as possible the initiative of the workers in their respective localities, the initiative displayed by the lower organisations of the Communist Parties and the labour movement in carrying out these decisions.

When leaving here the representatives of the revolutionary proletariat must bring to their respective countries the firm conviction that we Communists bear the responsibility for the fate of the working class, of the labour movement, the responsibility for the fate of each people, for the fate of all toiling humanity.

To us, the workers, and not to the social parasites and idlers, belongs the world—a world built by the hands of the workers. The present rulers of the capitalist world are but temporary rulers.

The proletariat is the real master, to-morrow's master of the world. And it must enter upon its historical rights, take into its hands the reins of government in every country, all over the world.

We are disciples of Marx and Engels, Lenin and Stalin. We should be worthy of our great teachers.

With Stalin at their head the millions of our political army, overcoming all difficulties and courageously breaking through all barriers, must and will level to the ground the fortress of capitalism and achieve the victory of socialism throughout the whole world!

Long live the unity of the working class!

Long live the Seventh World Congress of the Communist International!